WESTMAR COLL

P9-DFD-574

LIBRARY

Celsus
On The True Doctrine

A Discourse Against the Christians

Translated with a General Introduction
by R. Joseph Hoffmann

New York   Oxford
OXFORD UNIVERSITY PRESS
1987

89-372

Oxford University Press

Oxford   New York   Toronto
Delhi   Bombay   Calcutta   Madras   Karachi
Petaling Jaya   Singapore   Hong Kong   Tokyo
Nairobi   Dar es Salaam   Cape Town
Melbourne   Auckland

and associated companies in
Beirut   Berlin   Ibadan   Nicosia

Copyright © 1987 by Oxford University Press, Inc.

Published by Oxford University Press, Inc.,
200 Madison Avenue, New York, New York 10016

Oxford is a registered trademark of Oxford University Press

All rights reserved. No part of this publication may be reproduced,
stored in a retrieval system, or transmitted, in any form or by any means,
electronic, mechanical, photocopying, recording, or otherwise,
without the prior permission of Oxford University Press.

Library of Congress Cataloging-in-Publication Data

Celsus, Platonic philosopher, fl. 180.
   On the true doctrine.

   Translation of: Alēthēs logos.
   Bibliography: p.
   1. Christianity—Controversial literature.
2. Christianity and other religions—Roman.   3. Rome—
Religion.   4. Church history—Primitive and early church,
ca. 30-600.   I. Hoffmann, R. Joseph.   II. Title.
BR160.3.C4413   1987   230'.13   86-8619
ISBN 0-19-504150-X (alk. paper)
ISBN 0-19-504151-8 (pbk. : alk. paper)

9 8 7 6 5 4 3 2 1

Printed in the United States of America
on acid-free paper

To the Memory of
George Winsor MacRae, S.J.
Pastor et Magister

ACKNOWLEDGMENTS

Thanks are due the Horace H. Rackham School of Graduate Studies of the University of Michigan for providing a Faculty Fellowship to aid in the preparation of the present volume; to Ms. Carolyn Ruis of the University of Michigan Law School for her skillful proofreading of a moderately dense manuscript; to Ms. Paula Bouman for typing the manuscript; to the Theological Faculty, and especially to the Patristics Colloquium in the University of Oxford, for the initial discussions concerning the desirability of this project; and to my colleagues in the Department of Near Eastern Studies at the University of Michigan for the intellectual vigor that makes this sort of work possible and pleasurable.

Ann Arbor, Mich.   R.J.H.
Epiphany 1986

CONTENTS

LIST OF ANCIENT WORKS CITED

Unless otherwise noted, translations from biblical and other ancient writings are my own. In the interest of clarity, titles of the classical and patristic sources are given in English here and throughout the text, except in the case of works which are better known by their Greek or Latin names. The sources cited exist in a variety of standard editions and translations.

EARLY CHRISTIAN PSEUDEPIGRAPHA

The Apocryphon of John
The Epistle of Barnabas
The First Apocalypse of John
The Gospel of Thomas
Second Treatise of the Great Seth

CLASSICAL WRITINGS

Apollodorus of Athens, *The Library*
Apollonius, *Mirabilia*
Apuleius, *The Metamorphoses*
Cicero, *On the Nature of the Gods*
_____, *Tuscan Orations*
Diogenes Laertius, *Lives of the Philosophers*
Epictetus, *Discourses*

Euripides, *The Bacchantes*
———, *Phoenecian Maidens*
Galen, *On Appropriate Books*
Herodotus, *The History*
Iamblichus, *The Life of Pythagoras*
Josephus, *Against Apion*
———, *The Antiquities of the Jews*
———, *Wars of the Jews*
Lucian, *Alexander the False Prophet*
———, *The Death of Peregrinus*
———, *Imaginings*
Marcus Aurelius, *Meditations*
Philo of Alexandria, *On Husbandry*
———, *On Languages*
Plato, *Crito*
———, *Laws*
———, *Phaedo*
———, *Phaedrus*
———, *Politics*
———, *The Republic*
———, *The Seventh Letter*
———, *Theaetetus*
Pliny, *The Natural History*
Plotinus, *The Enneads*
Plutarch, *Lives of the Noble Greeks and Romans*
———, *Moralia*
Porphyry, *The Life of Plotinus*
———, *Pythagoras*
Seneca, *Epistles*
Suetonius, *The Twelve Caesars*
Tacitus, *The Annals of Imperial Rome*

PATRISTIC SOURCES

Clement of Alexandria, *An Exhortation to the Greeks*
———, *Miscellanies*

_____, *The Pedagogue*
Epiphanius of Salamis, *The Panarion, or Medicine Chest*
Eusebius, *Ecclesiastical History*
Hippolytus, *A Refutation of All Heresies*
Ignatius of Antioch, *The Epistle to the Ephesians*
_____, *The Epistle to the Romans*
Irenaeus, *Against Heresies*
Justin Martyr, *The First Apology*
Macarius the Great, *The Apocriticus*
Minucius Felix, *Octavius*
Origen of Alexandria, *Against Celsus**
_____, *Homily on the Book of Jeremiah*
Tertullian, *Against Marcion*
_____, *The Apology*
_____, *On the Flesh of Christ*
_____, *On Penitence*
_____, *On the Resurrection of the Flesh*
_____, *On the Soul*
_____, *The Prescription Against the Heretics*
_____, *To the Nations*

*References to the Chadwick translation of this work (Cambridge, Eng., 1953) are given in the text as *Origen, Contra Celsum.*

Celsus
ON THE TRUE DOCTRINE

General Introduction

I. ANTI-CHRISTIAN POLEMIC BEFORE CELSUS

Christianity was born of controversy. Not only the twenty-seven-book canon of writings but the individual books of the New Testament itself are charged with the spirit of contention and defense—so much, indeed, that a strong case may be made for seeing the canon as the earliest stratum in Christian apologetic literature.[1] Paul's own letters to wayward communities of Christian believers as far removed as Rome and Laodicaea suggest that the developing churches, themselves spewed into existence by the expulsion of heretical "Nazarenes" from the synagogues of Palestine, were called upon from an early date to defend themselves against Jewish and Greek detractors who made a mockery of the new, and to all seeming, eccentric messianic faith. As understood by the outsiders—Jew and Greek alike—the preaching of the Christian missionaries, centering on the humiliation and execution of a little-known Galilean rabbi, was either insanity or mere nonsense (I Cor. 1.23).

The very situation of the Christians in society, their perceived illegitimacy and the harrassment that followed from that perception, was a persuasive case against the merit of the claims they advanced on behalf of their Christ; yet they boasted of a continuity between his fate and their own rejection, and interpreted the syzygy with growing conviction as God's judgment on the "wisdom" of men (I Cor. 1.20f.). Only to "those who are perishing," Paul assured his converts, did the message seem foolish. "To those of us who are saved, it is nothing less than the power of God" (I Cor. 1.18).

5

It is not difficult to reconstruct the main lines in the development of early anti-Christian polemic from the writings preserved to us in the New Testament. And as these early themes are determinative for later polemists such as Celsus, Fronto, and Porphyry they may profitably be mentioned here.

I.1 THE APOCALYPTIC VISION AND ITS CONSEQUENCES

Christianity began as an apocalyptic movement of a specifically nondoctrinal sort. The earliest believers in Jesus were believers in a message of eschatological judgment, a message adumbrated not only in the teaching of a figure like John the Baptist and the monastic community at Khirbet Qumran, but widespread in the Hellenistic Judaism of the first century. Like other Jews of his generation, Jesus of Nazareth seems to have believed that history was moving toward catastrophe, toward a "Day of the Lord" when men would be called upon to answer for their sins. Escape from the impending judgment was possible, however, on condition that people repent of their sins. Thus, the message of the itinerant preacher known as John the Baptist: "You vipers' brood: who warned you to escape from the coming retribution? Then prove your repentance by the fruit it bears; and do not begin by saying to yourselves, 'We have Abraham for our father.' I tell you that God can make children for Abraham out of these stones here. Already the axe is laid to the roots of the trees; and every tree that fails to produce good fruit is cut down and thrown on the fire."[2]

Not different in kind from the message ascribed to John the Baptist, the gospel of Jesus centered on the joys and woes of the last days and the urgency entailed by the belief that the Son of Man[3] would descend to pronounce God's judgment even before Israel had been brought fully to repentance:

I tell you unashamedly: Some standing before me today will not have died before they see the power of God made manifest (Mark 9.1).

If you are persecuted in one place, run to another; but you will not get through the cities of Israel before the son of man comes (Matt. 10.23).

I tell you: this generation will not have passed away before the end of all is accomplished (Mark 13.30).

No less typical were the apocalyptic images used by Jesus and other wandering preachers to illustrate the urgency of their message: "On that day the man who is on the roof and his belongings in the house must not come down to pick them up; he, too, who is in the fields must not go back. Remember Lot's wife! Whoever seeks to save his life will lose it; whoever loses it will save it, and live." The day of the Son of Man would come suddenly—"like a thief in the night"—Paul assures his converts (I Thess. 5.2); yet its coming could be divined by watchful Christians through careful observance of the heavens and certain portents on earth. Thus, in the gospel attributed to Mark the uncertainty surrounding the time of the eschaton (cf. Mark 13.32) is mitigated by the knowledge that Jesus had forecast a variety of pre-eschatological events: the birth of false messiahs; an increase in wars; natural calamities; persecution of the cult for its beliefs; and dissension within families over childrens' apostasy from the faith of their fathers (Mark 13.6–12). With the exception of the natural disasters, most of the signs catalogued by Mark were events of the past by the time his gospel was composed, and their attribution to Jesus suggests the heightened sense of expectancy which characterizes the Christian view of history in the closing decades of the first century. Christianity was not alone in the production of messiahs; indeed, its Christ competed for converts with the christs of other apocalyptic sects, including the formidable cult of John the Baptist.

The "wars and rumours of wars" mentioned by the evangelist can be nothing other than a reference to the Roman incursions into Palestine, beginning in 66 C.E., and the "prophecy" that "not one stone (of the temple) will be left piled upon another" (Mark 13.2) must indicate that the devastation was complete before Mark set about writing his gospel (cf. Luke 21.20ff.).

The interrogation of Christians by synagogue councils and fairly erratic persecutions and expulsions of the cult from the Jewish congregations of the Diaspora—procedures for which there was no general rule or pattern[4]—were also widespread prior to the destruction of the Temple. A recollection that Jesus had envisaged such events and linked them specifically to the end of time would doubtless have had a consoling effect on a persecuted community, now set adrift to find its own religious way among the underground cults of the Roman *oikoumene*. Furthermore, it is certain that Christians living in Palestine at the close of the first century would have seen the destruction of the Temple as an indication of God's displeasure with the Jews and as a sign of their own long-awaited salvation, preceded by the return of Jesus in full regalia: "Then the son of man shall come in his glory, and his holy angels with him, and then shall he sit upon his throne of glory" (Matt. 25.31). The ruin of the Temple was thus interpreted as the beginning of the end-of-days; other signs, these to occur in the heavens, would appear (Mark 13.24–26, pars.), and the descent of the glorified Jesus in his capacity as judge of the unbelievers, the unrepentant, and the persecutors would immediately ensue.

Written when such expectation was at high pitch, the synoptic gospels grudgingly approve of the Roman punishment of Jewish zealotry, understanding the end of the Temple (abumbrated fictionally in the linking of Jesus' death on the cross with the rending of the veil of the temple in Mark 15.38, pars.) in eschatological terms as the beginning of a new covenant with a new Israel (Acts 4.10–12). The *leitourgia* itself, private banquets in Christian households, beyond the pale of synagogue surveillance, centered on the belief that the Lord was soon coming to finish what the Roman legions had started. In the celebration of the last supper of the disciples with their teacher, the hope was maintained that he would reappear to resume lordship of the community; indeed, the language they used and the tokens they offered were contrived to suggest his presence in the eucharist: "I am the bread of life . . . , the bread that has come from heaven so that by the eating of it a man may not die . . . If anyone eats of this bread, he will live forever: for this bread is my very flesh, the meat I give for the life of the world" (John 6.48f.).[5] For the expectant community, their attention riveted on the heavens for some sign of the reappearance of their savior, the eucharist was the interim realization of his presence and continuing care for his people, as well as a sacrament—an effective means—of symbolizing his promise to the church: "As often as you eat the bread and drink the cup, you are proclaiming the death of the Lord before he comes" (I Cor. 11.26).

1.2 CHALLENGES AND DEFENSIVE POSTURES

Jesus did not come, at least not in the way or at the time expected. Not surprisingly, therefore, the early opponents of the Christian cultus, doubtless beginning even before the expulsion of Christians from the synagogues, teased and finally harangued the believers for what was originally the cardinal tenet of the new religion: Jesus had been the Son of Man; unrecognized by his foes and misunderstood, now and again, by his closest associates, the message he preached was really a message about himself and his own coming. Indeed, it is not too much to say that the identification of Jesus as the eschatological Son of Man explicates, albeit not fully, the firmness of the belief in his resurrection; for if it was the case that the Son of Man was still to come, then it could not be the case that his death was final. Rather, it was a rite of passage leading to his glorification and triumph over the powers of sin and death. The gospels are notoriously circumspect in presenting Jesus' words about the Son of Man as first person discourses, but they are univocal in presenting his life story as the fulfillment of his own words concerning the *fate* of this apocalyptic figure: "He took the twelve aside and began to tell them what would happen to him, saying, 'Listen: we are on our way to Jerusalem, where the Son of Man will be delivered to the chief priests and the scribes; and they will deliver him to the gentiles after condemning him to death; they will mock him, scourge him, spit on him, and kill him. On the third day, he will rise again'" (Mark 10.32–34). It is certain in any case that whatever Jesus himself may have taught about the Son of Man and his coming, the early Christians were convinced that their own teacher would be the one—had been the one—designated by God to bring the old order to a close and that in virtue of this designation it was wrong to think of him merely as another Jewish victim of Roman justice.

The modification of Christian belief in the second coming is a separate chapter in the history of Christian thought and cannot be explored here in detail. It is sufficient to allude to Paul's words of consolation to Christians at Thessalonike, written perhaps in the fifties of the first century with a view to calming fears that the death of some believers nullified Paul's assurances that all who believed in his gospel would be "caught up to meet the Lord in the air" (I Thess. 4.17). Later Christians seem to have advanced a variety of inconsistent rationales for the delay: That the gospel must be preached and the conversion of the gentiles achieved before the end (Mark 13.10); that in advance of the last days the power of Rome, and of the emperor, must wane (doubt-

less envisaging the mundane corollary of the unseen celes-
tial battle between the powers of good and evil (Rom. 16.20;
II Thess. 2.2–10); that Jesus himself had professed ignorance about the exact time of the end (Mark 13.32); that
Jesus had refused to speculate about signs—an obviously
later stratum in the redaction of the gospel traditions and
one that plays havoc with the early eschatological discourses (Mark 8.11–12); or that the crucifixion itself marked
a transition from the old age to the new (cf. Luke 12.49–56;
17.22–37; Matt. 12.38–42).

We must see all of these rationales, strictly speaking, as
the defensive posture of a community challenged to provide evidence of its beliefs. The challenges—most of
which will have been issued in casual discussions between
Christians and Jews in the synagogues or in the marketplace, and perhaps later and more formally in synagogue tribunals such as we find romantically depicted in
the episode of Stephen's trial (Acts 8)—are not difficult to
reconstruct, and represent the earliest stratum in anti-
Christian polemical discourse.

By the early decades of the second century, the polemic
seems to have taken a literary turn, or so we may judge
from the apologetic literature written specifically to refute
the teachings of the church's early detractors. In the case
of the epistle ascribed to James (5.8), a figure especially
revered among Jewish Christians as being the biological
brother of Jesus, the persecution of Christians has caused
a general falling away from the church, or more precisely
from the eschatological vision that fired the hearts of earlier believers. By the time the so-called Second Letter of
Peter is written (not before 110), the apostasy has apparently become epidemic and seems to be encouraged by a
host of "scoffers"—probably Jewish and pagan writers
who point to the delay of the eschaton as proof that Christianity is a religion of falsehood. The writer (conceiting
himself as an aged Peter, "about to put off this earthly

tabernacle") calls upon the church to remember its early zeal. The tenor is through and through defensive: "For we have not followed cunningly devised fables when we revealed to you the power of our Lord Jesus Christ and his coming; indeed, we were eyewitnesses of his majesty" (II Peter 1.16). Using his "apostolic" rank as a weapon against nay-sayers, the writer complains of those who privately interpret scripture in a way uncongenial to Christian belief. Not only are such men unrighteous; they are positive libertines–adulterers, slanderers, asses speaking as though they were prophets (2.12ff.). Worse, it is clear that they (or some of them) are Christian believers (2.21) who have veered aside from the true faith at the urging of the skeptics.

What the skeptics taught is spelled out in some detail by the writer of the epistle: "Where now is the promise that he should come again? Since the first believers fell asleep, everything remains just as it was at the beginning of creation; nothing has changed" (II Pet. 3.4).

The author's reply sets the tone for Christian apologetic literature for decades to come: the attack, he asserts, is the work of those who love to scoff and to follow their own conceits. Their ignorance is the worse because it is deliberately contrived to subvert the word of God in prophecy and scripture (3.16f.), which they "twist to their own detriment."

1.3 ATTACKS ON CHRISTIAN MORALITY

The attack on Christian prophecy and the eschatological hopes of the community was pre-speculative, that is to say, it involved the most primitive level of Christian belief and was not, as such, an attack on doctrine or theological formulations. Nor was it primarily the effect of such attacks by anti-Christian polemists, but rather the yawning hiatus between hope and fulfillment that resulted in the gradual waning and eventual abandonment of the earliest form of belief in the Parousia. As Martin Werner has observed, "The whole of the first generation of the faithful died out without having experienced the fulfillment of the Pauline promise (of the eschaton), thus proving that it was certainly not the community of the saints of the last days. This meant that the apostolic age was not, in terms of the primitive Christian expectation, the beginning of the final epoch. But with the collapse of this presupposition of the definitive significance of the Apostolic Age went the eschatological significance of the death of Jesus. This change of things proved itself in effect to be the turning point of that subsequent crisis of Christianity which, starting in the postapostolic period, led by virtue of the process of hellenization to early Catholicism."[6]

Thus while it cannot be said that the rhetorical sallies of pagan and Jewish critics had much to do with the waning of enthusiasm, the loss of the early generations of Christians vitiated any attempt to explain the apocalyptic stratum of Christian belief to those already disposed to look mistrustfully at the new religion.

Moreover, enthusiasm itself, as a response to the Christian view of history as a clock on the verge of stopping, was a persistent and embarrassing problem for the early church. Paul writes to correct a rather virulent form of this enthusiasm at Corinth in the fifties, laboring against the odds to root out "such immorality as is not even found among the pagans" (I Corinthians 5.1). Its corollaries— factionalism, gluttony, competition for the outpouring and demonstration of spiritual gifts (charismata) in the form of prophecy and ecstatic utterance (I Cor. 11–15)— cannot have been limited to Corinth, however. The epistle attributed in the New Testament to Jude and written in the last years of the first century indicates the pestiferousness of the problem well after Paul's valiant efforts to curb ecstaticism and sexual license in certain congregations. The author of "Jude's" epistle writes to imprecate those who "walk in the way of Cain and abandon themselves to Balaam's error and perish in Korah's rebellion" (Jude 11). The references clearly point to internal disarray and perhaps to a growing libertinism within the churches: Cain typified treachery, lust, avarice, and self-indulgence for first-century writers;[7] Balaam's error (Numbers 22–24) was covetousness and the corruption of the young; the reference to Khora's rebellion (Num. 16.1–34; Josephus, *Antiquities,* 4.2.), is to the enemies of Moses who were thought to have descended live into Sheol. The last of the references would indicate that the source of the troubles is a group of agitators who advocate pleasure in the here and now as a part of their love feasts: "They concern themselves with the things of the flesh and thus corrupt themselves" (Jude 10).

Eschatological thinking thus seems to have bred both an ascetic form of piety, best represented in Paul's letters (Rom. 6.12–15; I Cor. 6.10–19) and stemming from the conviction that, as the present order is corrupt, one ought to defy the world through self-mortification and disregard of the flesh, and an antinomian enthusiasm, one aspect of which was sexual self-indulgence. These responses to the eschaton, in turn, correspond to rival theological outlooks in the early church: the antinomian emphasis, favored especially by some of Paul's converts, took its cue from Paul's (and doubtless other missionaries') stance against the law. Without the constraints of the Jewish law, such Christians reasoned, anything is possible; and as the Christian is saved by grace and faith rather than by works, anything is permissible. Given the terms of his message to the churches, Paul cannot really dispute such logic. But its practical consequences in primarily gentile congregations must have been obvious to him from an early date. Thus we find him admonishing the Christian community in Rome—one he knows only by report—that the law is holy, just, and good (Rom. 7.12), though it is not to be confused with the means of salvation. From Paul's reproaches, we can gather that he meant to deprive the Roman Christians of their illusions about the meaning of the gospel: "We are not so poor, I should hope, that we must live for the flesh; for if we live for the flesh we shall die; but if we live through the spirit and deny the cravings of the flesh we shall live" (Rom. 8.12–13). The ascetic response, represented by Paul himself and shared by the Jewish sectarians at Qumran and at least some gnostic Christians, originated in the apocalyptic view that the material world is laden with encumbrances to salvation. The desires of the flesh and the procreation of the human race that accrues to such desire were inimical to the imagined purposes of the God who would "create a new heaven and a new earth," and who had declared the old order and the travails of old times at an end (Isa. 65.17f.).

Although church fathers like Irenaeus and Tertullian argue against the asceticism of such groups as the Encratites, the Marcionites, and assorted gnostic sects, they did not manage successfully to turn the tide away from the opposite shore, namely the libertinism normally associated with the salvation cults of the empire. As we have noted, salvationism had imprinted itself on the Christian church at Corinth by the fifties of the first century; by the end of the century, the author of the letter attributed to James offers an already archaic solution—the doing of works (2.14)—as an antidote to the salvation-by-faith doctrine advocated by Paul in his desperate attempts to bring the churches under moral control. By the early decades of the second century, however, the alliance between Christianity and the mystery religions was accomplished fact; indeed, the description of the first eucharist in the gospel of Mark shows clearly the cultic modification of what seems to have originated as a Passover celebration by Jesus and his followers, and the gospel of John (6.51–58) makes the association of the eucharist with the mysteries explicit: Jesus there becomes the sacramental bread of life that guarantees immortality and resurrection to the initiates. Ignatius of Antioch does not hesitate to speak of the eucharist as the *pharmakon tes zoēs,* the "medicine of immortality";[8] "Not as common bread and common drink do we receive these," Justin Martyr insists, "[but as] food which is blessed by the prayer of his word and from which our blood and flesh by transmutation are nourished."[9]

As we may gather from the report of the Younger Pliny to the emperor Trajan,[10] written around 111, rumors of Christian excesses were widespread throughout Asia Minor and were doubtless linked in the popular mind with the nocturnal forest rites of the Bacchae. Described by Livy during the reign of Augustus (27 B.C.E.–14 C.E.) these rites were thought to include drunkenness, the defilement of women, promiscuous intercourse, and assorted other debaucheries. Pliny had heard this much and more about the clandestine practices of the Christians— including suggestions that they occasionally sacrificed and ate their young and indulged in ritual incest at their love banquets. Pliny himself appears to credit the Christian denial of such charges ("They claim . . . they meet to partake of food, but food of an ordinary and innocent kind"), at the same time professing a healthy ignorance about their beliefs. Other observers of roughly the same period were not so indifferent. The Latin rhetorician Marcus Cornelius Fronto (100–166?) described the feasts of the Christians (perhaps the Carpocratians mentioned by Clement of Alexandria)[11] as abominations and affronts to the Roman sense of decency:

> A young baby is covered over with flour, the object being to deceive the unwary. It is then served before the person to be admitted to the rites. The recruit is urged to inflict blows onto it [which] appear to be harmless because of the covering of flour. Thus the baby is killed with wounds that remain unseen and concealed. It is the blood of this infant—I shudder to

mention it—it is this blood that they lick with thirsty lips; the limbs they distribute eagerly; this is the victim by which they seal the covenant.[12]

Fronto offers an equally full description of the supposed incestuous passions of the Christian congregations:

> On a special day they gather in a feast with all their children, sisters, mothers all sexes and ages. There, flushed with the banquet after such feasting and drinking, they begin to burn with incestuous passions. They provoke a dog tied to the lampstand to leap and bound towards a scrap of food which they have tossed outside the reach of his chain. By this means the light is overturned and extinguished, and with it common knowledge of their actions; in the shameless dark and with unspeakable lust they copulate in random unions, all being equally guilty of incest, some by deed but everyone by complicity.[13]

Justin Martyr, Tertullian, and Epiphanius, to name but three early Christian writers, know of Christian groups of various provenances that engage in comparably bizarre rites. Epiphanius points to an obscure sect called by him the Phibionites, who

> unite with each other [sister and brother] in the passion of fornication. . . . The woman and the man take the fluid of the emission of the man into their hands, they stand, turn toward heaven, their hands besmeared by uncleanness, and pray (saying) "We offer to thee this gift, the body of Christ," and then they eat it, their own ugliness, and say: "This is the body of Christ and this is the Passover for the sake of which our bodies suffer and are forced to confess the suffering of Christ." Similarly also with the woman when she happens to be in the flowing of the blood, they gather the blood of menstruation of her uncleanness and eat it together and say, "This is the blood of Christ."[14]

The earliest literary polemic against the Christian associations was thus directed against the antinomian and libertine congregations of the new religious diaspora. Countervailing and mediating tendencies must have existed side by side with the more extreme forms of salvationism and enthusiasm, and the early writers are anxious to deflect attacks on the libertine sects by insisting that they have falsely laid claim to the name "Christian": "We demand that those accused to you be judged in order that each one who is convicted may be punished as an evildoer and not as a Christian."[15] This process of differentiation, together with its theological and doctrinal corollaries, is of inestimable importance in guaging the emergence of Christian "orthodoxy" or "right belief"; for it is in the effort to correct an impression given by the extremist movements that the articulation of opposing systems of belief comes into focus. So too does the obverse: who believes wrongly—namely the heretics—may be expected to behave wrongly.[16]

It is impossible to measure the extent of the alleged abuses of the Christian mystery, but certain that by Tertullian's day (145–220) suspicion of the new religion was widespread and a favorite topos for literary invective. "Not two hundred and fifty years have passed since our life began," Tertullian writes in the *Ad nationes*, "yet the rumors that circulate against us, anchored in the cruelty of the human mind, enjoy considerable success. . . . If the Tiber has overflowed its banks, or if the Nile has remained in its bed, if the sky has been still or the earth has been disrupted, if plague has killed or famine struck, your cry is, 'Let the Christians have it!'"[17] Among the charges reported against the Christians in his *Apology*, Tertullian mentions murder, cannibalism, treason, sacrilege (atheism), and incest—crimes already envisaged in Justin's *apologia* and perhaps also by the author of I Peter 2.12 (*katalalousin hymon hos kakopoion:* "[the nations] . . . speak against you as evildoers"). A more general "crime" is the clannishness of the Christian communities and their disregard for the clubs, religious associations, and entertainments of ordinary citizens. To this Tertullian responds in detail:

We are a body knit together by a common religious profession, by unity of discipline, and by the bond of common hope. We meet together as an assembly and congregation, that, offering up prayer to God as with united force we may wrestle with him in our supplications: This violence God delights in. We pray for the emperors, too—for their ministers and for all in authority, for the welfare of the world, for the prevalence of peace and for the delay of the final consummation. We assemble to read our sacred writings, if any peculiarity of the times makes either forewarning or reminiscence needful. . . . In the same place also exhortations are made, rebukes and sacred censures are administered. . . . Though we have our treasure chest, it is not made up of purchase money. . . . Our gifts are, as it were, piety's deposit. For they are not taken and spent on feasts and drinking bouts and eating-houses, but to support and bury poor people, to supply the wants and needs of boys and girls destitute of parents, and of old persons confined to the house.[18]

Tertullian goes on to describe the meaning of the Christian love feast, where

a peculiar respect is paid to the lowly . . . as it is an act of religious service, it permits no vileness or immodesty. The participants, reclining, taste first of a prayer to God. As much is eaten as satisfies the craving of hunger; as much is drunk as befits the chaste. . . . They talk as though the Lord were listening; and after washing their hands and bringing in candles each is asked to stand forth and sing, as it were, a hymn to God—one from scripture or one of his own composing (a proof of the measure of his drinking!). As the feast commenced with prayer, so with prayer it is closed. We go from it not like troops of evildoers nor bands of vagabonds, nor to break out into licentious acts, but to have as much care for our modesty and chastity as if we had been at a seminar on virtue rather than at a banquet.[19]

Tertullian's description of the *agape* does nothing to exclude the possibility of abuses, and indeed his analogies— the feasts of the Apaturia, the Bacchae, the Attic mysteries, and the cult of Serapis—suggest that the feasts were often marred by explosions of enthusiasm. These were to be tolerated on Tertullian's reckoning because the banquets, despite their cost, benefited the needy and because Christians were entitled (like the Megarians) "to feast as though they were going to die on the morrow." In any event, it is obvious from the direction of his argument that outsiders were fond of pointing out inconsistencies in the Christian public attitude toward pagan "licentiousness" and their private indulgences in wine and song.

It is probable that the earliest pagan critics of Christianity were most troubled by the seeming incoherence of the Christian position toward society and toward the recognized religions of the state. From Justin's time, and doubtless before, it was common for Christians to insist on their exclusive right to salvation, their indestructibility ("The oftener we are mown down by you, the more we grow"[20]), their antiquity, the superiority of their ethic, and the uniqueness of their religious forms. To the pagan intellectual of the second century, as for Celsus, these were intolerable and unwarranted assumptions—contradicted indeed by everything one knew about Roman civilization and its antecedents and by everything one wanted to believe about Roman morality, justice, and religion. Were one to try to account for the increasing viciousness of the attacks on Christian morality between the time of Justin and Tertullian's day, one would have to say that its precondition was the common perception among Roman intellectuals that the Christians, in despising the rituals and conventions of imperial civilization, possessed no basis or standard by which to measure the morality of their actions. So widespread was this perception that confessing Christians were sometimes coaxed by their accusers to eat sausages stuffed with raw animal viscera as proof of their fondness for human blood.[21]

By their own accounting people who paid "no vain or foolish honours to the emperor—men who believe in the true religion and prefer to celebrate their festal days with good conscience instead of with common wantonness"— the Christians came more and more to be regarded by their observers as public enemies,[22] a third race, given to infanticide[23] and onocoetism (ass worship).[24] The predictable consensus of the apologists, following from their equally predictable evaluation of a lump of pagan practices, was that the Christians alone were good, pure, and truthful—"We alone are without crime . . . taught by God himself what goodness is, we have both a perfect knowledge of it as revealed to us by a perfect master, and we faithfully do his will, as enjoined on us by a judge we dare not despise. But your ideas of virtue you have got from mere human authority, and on human authority too its obligations rest: hence your system of practical morality is deficient."[25]

Combined with their provocative contempt for the moral philosophy of the empire was a certain elegiac attitude toward imperial religion. Christianity had not only begun to displace the gods, the apologists calculated, but it had proved them false and reduced them to the level of pious superstition. "Do not seek out the profane basin, the tripod of Cirra or the brazen cauldron of Dodona. . . . The spring of Castalia has fallen silent, so has that of Colophon. . . . Tell us now of that other prophecy, or rather madness, of the untruthful oracles, those of Aohiarius and Amphilocus, and then place next to Pythian Apollo . . . interpreters of dreams and those possessed by spirits."[26]

In his *Exhortation to the Greeks* (1.1) Clement alleges that the pagans give credence to worthless legends: "Orpheus and the Theban and the Methymnian too are not worthy (even) of the name man, since they were deceivers and under cover of music outraged human life—being influenced by demons, through some artful sorcery, to compass man's ruin." The pagans commemorate "deeds of violence" in their religious rites, and with "sticks and stones, statues and pictures they build up the stupidity of custom" (2.2). They worship Dionysus with orgies in which they celebrate their sacred frenzy with a feast of raw flesh; similarly savage are the rites associated with the cults of Demeter, Corybantes, and Eleusis. For Clement, the point to be derived from the excesses of the mystery religions was perfectly obvious:

> The mysteries are mere custom and vain opinion. It is a deceit of the serpent that men worship when they turn with spurious piety towards these sacred initiations that are really profanities and solemn rites without sanctity. . . . What manifest shame-lessness! Formerly, night which drew a veil over the pleasure of temperate men, was a time for silence. But now, when night is for those who are being initiated, a temptation for licentious talk abounds, and the torch fires convict unbridled pas-sions. . . . Ah! Suffer night to hide the mysteries. Let the orgies be honored by darkness.[27]

Like Justin and his near contemporary, Tertullian, Clement contrasts the true mystery with the false rites of the unbelievers, the true gnosis with the false doctrines of the pagans. The Christians had been branded atheists for their refusal to pay homage to the recognized gods of the state; Clement expropriates the charge and turns it against the critics: "I am right in branding as atheists men who are ignorant of the true God but who shamefully worship a child being torn to pieces by Titans—a poor grief-stricken woman, and parts of the body which from a sense of shame are truly too sacred to speak of."[28] Clement (again like Tertullian, *Apology,* 11.) offers as proof of this "athe-ism" the fact that the gods were really men who lived and worked on earth; their divine stature is merely honorific (2.2.24) as can be seen from the "countless host of mortal and perishable men who have been called by the names of the [gods]."[29] They were born not of virgins but of human mothers later elevated, in virtue of their sons' reputations, to the level of goddess; furthermore, in their passions, jealousies, battles, wounds, sexual cravings, and misfortunes, they betrayed their human origins. At least a portion of Clement's critique of the evolution of the gods was of considerable use to the pagan opponents of Christianity, who could argue (as does Celsus) that the Christians worshipped as a god a man of rather insignificant proportions.

So many of Clement's central themes appear in the pagan moral critiques of Christianity that one cannot avoid the impression that the polemic, on both sides, became thematically stereotyped from an early date: If the pagans were atheists because they worshipped the wrong god or too many gods, the Christians were atheists for rejecting the approved gods of the empire and refusing to recognize the divinity of the emperor; if the pagan mysteries were marred by immorality, the Christian cultus had ritualized incest and gluttony; if the Bacchantes in their frenzy sometimes cannibalized outsiders, the Christians for their part indulged in Thyestean banquets and drank the blood of innocent children.[30] Just as there was nothing exclusive about the symbols and myths employed by the Christians in their celebrations, so there was nothing exclusive about the charges each side laid at the other's door: "The things you do openly and with applause," writes Justin concerning the exposure of children, "these you lay to our charge, which in truth does no harm to us, who shrink from doing any such things, but only to those who do them and who bear false witness against us" (*First Apology*, 27).

In arguing for the moral superiority of Christianity and defending its claim to possess the only key to salvation, the apologists precipitated a long history of polemical squabbling remarkable primarily for the banality of its content. In the course of the battle, Christian writers habitually insisted on the originality of their beliefs and rites, whilst at the same time arguing vigorously for the antiquity of their religion—its adumbration in Hebrew prophecy and song, in Greek myth and philosophy, and even in the perverse rites it had come to supplant. Any real comparison between Christianity and paganism became, after Justin's day, an impossibility as the argument became fixed that the Christian religion was both the fulfillment of ancient expectations and the true religion whose perfection was foreseen and preemptively imitated by the demons,

> For having heard it proclaimed through the prophets that the Christ was to come and that the ungodly among men were to be punished by fire [the wicked spirits] put forward many to be called sons of Jupiter, under the impression that they would be able to produce in men the idea that the things that were said with regard to Christ were merely marvellous tales, like the things that were said by the poets.[31]

II. PAGAN OPPOSITION: FROM MORAL
TO INTELLECTUAL CRITIQUE

The moral critiques of Christianity antedate the philosophical assaults of writers like Celsus for an obvious reason: the Christianity of the first century had yet to develop an assailable system of belief or a fixed canon of writings from which such beliefs could be educed. It is only as doctrine begins to supplant apocalyptic enthusiasm and the practices associated with it that the focus of pagan writers shifts from what Christians do to what they teach, from the occasional excesses of the love feasts to the gospel story and its religious implications. Tacitus and Pliny, the first writers to take notice of Christianity, speak of the religion with social disdain as *exitiabilis superstitio, prava et immodica superstitio,* and *inflexibilis obstinatio,* that is, the Christians were superstitious fanatics given to outpourings of enthusiasm. According to Tacitus, they were haters of humanity, and according to Crescens, a cynic philosopher of the mid-second century, they were both impious and atheistic. All of these early critiques lack teeth. Based almost certainly on casual impressions and hearsay, they reflect the common Roman distaste for what is new and unapproved, but tell us very little about what particulars of the new religion the opponents found objectionable.

II.1 LUCIAN

This situation changes dramatically in the middle decades of the second century. The rhetorician Lucian, born at Samosata (Syria) in 120, regarded Christianity as a form of sophistry aimed at an unusually gullible class of people— a criticism later exploited by the philosopher Celsus (*Against Celsus*, 3.44). The members of the new sect worship "a crucified sophist," an epithet which suggests the influence of Jewish views of Christianity on pagan writers.[32] In line with the popular impression of the social and philosophical shortcomings of the new religion, Lucian characterized the sectarians as men and women of a distinctly unphilosophical cast, ready at the drop of a hat to enthrone new prophets and leaders.

Such is the case with his mock-cynic philosopher-turned-Christian priest, Peregrinus Proteus (169). After a profligate youth during which he is said to have undergone "a thousand transformations," Peregrinus turns to "the priests and scribes of the Christians" and becomes an expert in "that astonishing religion they have":

> Naturally in no time at all he had them looking like babies and had become their prophet, leader, head of the synagogue, and what not all by himself. He expounded and commented on their sacred writings and even authored a number himself. They looked up to him as a god, made him their lawgiver, and

put his name down as the official patron of the sect, or at least
vice patron, second to that man they still worship today, the
one who was crucified in Palestine because he brought this
new cult into being.[33]

Lucian here satirizes the ease of preferment which a
reasonably clever man like Peregrinus finds available to
him among the unlettered. Within a short time the philosopher enjoys a status second only to the "founder" himself—an obvious reference to the speed with which Jesus
was catapulted into significance by his followers. Like
Jesus, he is proclaimed a god; like Jesus, he is arrested for
his teachings, "an event which set him up for his future
career." While the Christians consider this arrest a tragedy
(so, too, the Apostles, apud. Mark 10.32–33), Peregrinus
thereby acquires "status, a magic aura, and the public
notice he was so passionately in love with."[34] There seems
little doubt that the worst instincts of Peregrinus are contrived to invite comparison with the chicanery of Jesus,
the deceiver who used magical arts to attract disciples and
lead Israel into apostasy.

Lucian goes on to lampoon the response of the Christians to the arrest of Peregrinus in language that reveals
something about their loyalties and practices; above all, it
is clear from his description that the claims made by Christian writers like Justin Martyr and Luke on behalf of the
communalism of the sect are not altogether exaggerated.
Their loyal devotion to an imprisoned member, their care
for widows and orphans, their worship of their founder,
their indifference to worldly interests and to martyrdom
itself, and their settled belief in immortality are mentioned—with patronizing contempt, it is true, but yet as
well-known characteristics of the Christian brotherhood:

From the crack of dawn you could see grey-haired widows and
orphan children hanging around the prison, and the bigwigs
of the sect used to bribe the jailers so they could spend the

night with (Peregrinus) inside. Full-course dinners were brought to him, their holy scriptures read to him, and our excellent Peregrinus . . . was hailed as a latter-day Socrates. From as far away as Asia Minor Christian communities sent committees, paying their expenses out of the common funds to help him with advice and consolation. . . . And so, because Peregrinus was in jail, money poured in from them; he picked up a very nice income this way. You see, for one thing the poor devils have convinced themselves that they are all going to be immortal and live forever, which makes most of them take death lightly and voluntarily give themselves up to it. For another, that first lawgiver of theirs persuaded them that they're all brothers the minute they deny the Greek gods (thereby breaking our law) and take to worshipping him—the crucified sophist himself, and to living their lives according to his rules. They scorn all possessions without distinction and treat them as community property; doctrines such as these they accept strictly on faith. Consequently, if a professional sharper who knows how to capitalize on a situation gets among them, he makes himself a millionaire overnight, laughing up his sleeve at the simpletons.[35]

II.2 FURTHER CRITIQUES

The criticism of Christianity for its lack of a coherent philosophical system—a criticism which cannot easily be separated from the sociomoral attacks on the sort of people who found the new religion appealing—becomes a fixture of the pagan polemical writings from the mid-second century onward. Celsus himself, in an overfamous passage, alleges that most Christians "do not want to give or receive a reason for what they believe" but rather win converts by telling them "not to ask questions but to have faith."[36] Nor was the philosophical inadequacy of the new religion something known only to outsiders. Christian teachers too were divided over the extent to which the sacred books, unsupported by theological premises, argument, and definition, were sufficient to the task of displaying the beliefs of the new religion. Toward the end of the second century, the Christian teacher Rhodo is able to scoff at a pious Marcionite bishop by the name of Apelles for no better reason than that he "used to say that it is not necessary to investigate an argument fully and that each should remain in his own belief; for he asserted that those who placed their hope in the crucified would be saved."[37]

As a rule, the pagan critics of the later second century, Celsus included, are critics of Christian credulity, not of Christian creeds. Their attitude is summarized in Suetonius' characterization of the new religion as a *superstitio nova ac malefaca,* a cult without the redeeming virtues of the old religions;[38] in Epictetus' opinion,[39] that the Christians were driven to martyrdom (in imitation of their master) by blind fanaticism; and in Marcus Aurelius' (ca. 170)[40] stoical disregard for Christian "suicide": "Readiness to die must come from a man's own judgment, not from mere obstinacy as with the Christians; it must come considerately and in such a way [as to persuade others that death is not horrible], not with tragic displays." In the second century, Christian missionaries were yet in the habit of preaching the Christ of Paul, Marcion, and Apelles: the gospel of a man who had once taught in Galilee and Judea, who had been unrecognized by his own people during his public ministry, who had been crucified as an outlaw, raised from the dead and appointed to divine sonship by the supreme God.

If there was nothing exactly new in such a story—Rome had inherited its savior myths from far and wide—the reenactment of its details by the Christian brotherhood was an easy target for ridicule. Like the founder, the Christians were homeless preachers who made what little money they needed from their revivals; like the founder, and like Paul, they led a life fraught with danger; rejection was their common lot; as fools for Christ, they embraced the fate of Jesus willingly, in the certainty that his triumph was their triumph and that they would be raised up on the last day. At best, such emulation might be seen as foolhardiness or, to use the common epithet, "superstition." Certain second-century onlookers, Galen being the most celebrated,[41] were willing to make concessions for the fideism of the Christians because, after all, "Most people are unable to follow any demonstrative argument consecutively and hence need parables and benefit from them, just as now we see these people called 'Christians' drawing their faith from parables and miracles, and yet sometimes acting in the same way as those who practice philosophy." Since any philosophical position must, on Galen's terms, residuate in a moral life, the parables and myths of the Christians, however feeble in strictly intellectual terms, ought not to be judged too harshly. Yet Galen too is critical of any "school" that teaches its adherents to accept everything on faith, "as the followers of Moses and Christ teach theirs."[42]

III. CELSUS

Of the early critics of the Christian church, the Greek philosopher Celsus (ca. 185) is at once the most accessible and the most eclectic. He is accessible because his eloquent opponent, Origen of Alexandria, quotes from Celsus' *On the True Doctrine* in generous measure; hence it is possible to reconstruct the main lines of the philosopher's argument in detail. This is not true in the case of the church's most vigorous (and in some ways more learned) third-century opponent, Porphyry, whose fifteen books against the Christians (*The Philosophy from Oracles*) were burned by order of the emperors Theodosius II and Valentinian III in 448 and are known chiefly through quotations in the works of the church fathers.[43] At the same time, Celsus' discourse shows him to be an eclectic philosopher—a dabbler in various schools of thought, including Platonism and Stoicism, and a student of history and the religious customs of many nations.

Celsus is silent concerning the supposed immorality of the Christians, a fact which may suggest his disbelief of such reports or his preference for a higher level of discussion. However that may be, in attacking the beliefs of the Christian community on a philosophical plane he raises the level of discussion on the Christian side from apology to argument. And despite his repetitious contempt for the low intellectual attainment of Christian teachers and presbyters, the very extent of his essay demonstrates the seriousness with which the new religion was taken in the closing decades of the second century.[44]

III.1 THE IDENTITY OF CELSUS

The identity of Celsus is a subject for educated conjecture. Keim argued[45] that he was a friend of Lucian of Samosata, whose satirical view of Christianity we have discussed (see pp. 25–27). Origen himself tells us[46] that Celsus has been dead "for a long time,"[47] and elsewhere (1.8) indefinitely assigns him to "Hadrian's time and later," in contrast to another Epicurean philosopher called Celsus who lived during Nero's reign (54–68 C.E.). A succession of scholars has found Origen's dating of Celsus' activity—the thirties of the second century—rather too early, a majority preferring to place him in the sixties or seventies. Such reading between the lines is justifiable in view of Origen's confusion about who Celsus was. Galen[48] mentions having addressed a letter to "Celsus the Epicurean," a man who had written several books against magic, and Lucian dedicates his *Alexander, the False Prophet,* a work in which Christianity comes in for passing mention in connection with Epicureanism,[49] to a certain Celsus, who "has gone into the subject [of magic and magicians] sufficiently and presented ample material . . . in (his) exposé of magicians, an excellent and most useful work which should pound sense into whoever opens it."[50] Objections to the identification of the Celsus of Origen's treatise with the philosophical opponent of magicians known to Galen and to Lucian have centered on the consideration—brought out fully by Chadwick— that Origen's Celsus "is very far from being in any sense an Epicurean. His philosophy is middle Platonism and with Epicureanism he betrays no affinities at all."[51] The assumption would be that Origen, being led astray by Ambrose, at whose invitation he penned his refutation, inferred Celsus' Epicureanism[52] from his knowledge of Galen's correspondence with the author of several books against magic.[53] For his part, however, Origen finds Celsus simply an inconsistent Epicurean, one who for convenience' sake is ready to suppress certain dogmas in the interest of defeating the dogmas of the opposition:

> From other writings, he is found to be an Epicurean; but here [i.e., in reference to Christian martyrdom] because he appears to have more reasonable grounds for criticising Christianity if he does not confess the doctrines of Epicurus he pretends (to embrace another view). . . . He knew that if he admitted he was an Epicurean he would not be worthy of credit in his criticisms of those who in some way introduce a doctrine of providence and who set a God over the universe.[54]

Theodor Keim, in seeking to restore Celsus' *True Doctrine,* credited Origen's opinion, arguing that Celsus was not a full-blooded Epicurean[55] but rather an eclectic Platonist. And more recently Robert Wilken has advanced the point that "to pin the label 'Epicurean' on Celsus (was to) make the task of criticism easier."[56] We need only consider Tertullian's meaningless castigation of Marcion's epicurean tendencies[57] to see that the term was thrown about rather loosely in religious controversy and probably was meant to suggest atheism and disregard for social custom and popular religion.[58] Such at least is the use made of

Epicurus' name in the valedictory of *Alexander, the False Prophet*, where Lucian mentions Celsus' love for the truth as the foremost epicurean virtue, in sharp contrast to the sham displays of the deceptive hero of his tale.[59] Further, there are a number of similarities between Lucian's friend and Origen's opponent. One cannot help but notice that both are said to be ardently opposed to magic, Lucian's friend having written a number of treatises against magicians,[60] Origen's adversary charging off the miracles of Jesus to magical practices that were learned by his disciples.[61] If one accepts that both Lucian and Celsus "the Epicurean" shared a like disregard for the doings of charlatans and the gullibility of religious folk, and found Christianity especially susceptible of criticism in this regard,[62] then there is little reason to assume that Lucian and Origen address different philosophers in their works. Moreover, as Lucian's friend lived under Commodus (ca. 180) and Origen's opponent wrote around 177–80,[63] or during the persecuting reign of Marcus Aurelius, there is no reason on strictly chronological grounds to argue their separate identities. In the end, any decision is likely to center on whether the Celsus of Origen's work is or is not an "Epicurean," and while it is true that epicurean opinions are not in bold relief in the passages cited in the *Contra Celsum*, we must consider (a) that Origen provides only extracts from Celsus' work; (b) that Celsus' work may have been penned *after* the conversion from Epicureanism that Origen envisages (4.54), thus explaining (c) that Celsus' Epicureanism is thought by Origen "to be proved [not from his work against the Christians] but from other books" (1.8), presumably written before the *Alēthēs Logos*. In any event, the undeniable fact that the Celsus of Origen's apology shows a preference for middle Platonism does not exclude the possibility that he is the Celsus of Lucian's satire. The best guess is that the *True Doctrine* was written in the last quarter of the second century, probably, as Keim supposes, during the persecutions at Lyon and Vienne (177) following the rescript of Marcus Aurelius.[64]

III.2 THE ARGUMENT

The great church historian Philip Schaff described Celsus' *True Doctrine* as "superficial, loose, and lightminded . . . striking proof of the inability of natural reason to under- stand Christian truth."[65] The treatise had, Schaff com- plained, "no savour of humility, no sense of the corrup- tion of human nature and man's need of redemption; it is full of heathen passion and prejudice, utterly blind to any spiritual realities."[66] Such evaluations bespeak the apolo- getic tendencies of a now outmoded historiographical school. Yet Schaff rightly perceived that Celsus' argu- ments against Christianity are curiously modern: "He em- ploys all the aids which the culture of his age afforded, all the weapons of learning, common sense, wit, sarcasm, and dramatic animation of style to disprove Christianity; and he anticipates most of the arguments and sophisms of the deists and infidels of later times."[67] More recent eval- uations of Celsus' work have focused on his basic conser- vatism. His attack on Christianity is not, as Carl Andresen suggested, a planless polemic but rather "is written from a consistent point of view, and his rejection of the Christian movement arises out of his views about the society in which he lives, the intellectual and spiritual traditions that animated his society, and the religious convictions on which it was based."[68] In short, Celsus may be regarded as a defender of the old order and its religious values, one who regarded Christianity as a potentially seditionist cult, retailing new ideas that seemed to him unwarranted mod- ifications of old doctrines.[69]

Celsus' assualt on Christianity was not prompted by distemper or a failure to discern God's plan for the world in the new religion. Rather, he "sensed that Christians had severed the traditional bond between religion and a 'nation' or people"[70] in an age when religious traditions were widely held to express a people's continuity with the past and their national allegiance to constituted authority. Tertullian boasts, indeed, that Christians "pay no vain, nor false, nor foolish, honours to the emperor; that as men believing in the *true* religion they prefer to celebrate their festival days with a good conscience";[7]for this reason, he says pridefully, "they are counted as public enemies— enemies of humanity—a 'third race' of men."[72] It is the sentiment behind Tertullian's boasting that would have been the most galling to the likes of Celsus: Here was an upstart cult that not only bragged about its numbers but actually called the old ways to the dock;[73] that arrogated to itself the reason for the duration of the empire[74] and even claimed that without Christians in every city to serve as subjects, the emperor would find himself without a people to rule.[75] "Take care, lest those whom you call the third race should obtain the first rank, since there is no nation indeed which is not Christian. Whatever nation therefore was the first, is nevertheless Christian now."[76] Here was a religious association, however extensive by Tertullian's calculations, behaving like a nation, lacking a nation's history and traditions, yet binding its membership by allegiance to traditions and history of its own making. It is hardly surprising to find a conservative philosopher like Celsus reminding the Christians that their security and wellbeing come at a price: "If everyone were to adopt the Christian's attitude, there would be no rule of law; legitimate authority would be abandoned; earthly things would return to chaos and come into the hands of the lawless and savage barbarians—and nothing further would be heard of Christian worship and wisdom anywhere in the world. Indeed, for your superstition to persist, the power of the emperor is necessary."[77] The whole of Celsus' treatise must be viewed with his overriding purpose—the defense of tradition and authority—in mind.

• Celsus begins his attack by defending the proscription of Christianity throughout the empire: The members of the association huddle together in secret "for fear of being found out and brought to trial." Like the adherents of other secret associations, the Christians take advantage of the gullible and the uneducated in order to propagate their religion, neither giving nor demanding any reasons for their beliefs. Celsus states that his purpose in refuting them is to show them the true character of their religion and the sources of their opinions. This he proceeds to do, first of all, by pointing up the unoriginality of Christian doctrine in great detail, arguing that the immediate source of the Christian religion, Judaism, is one *historia* among many; it cannot be universalized nor made normative for the reason that it offers but one perspective, and that an imperfect one, of the world and its origins. Yet Judaism shares with other great civilizations some awareness of that true and ancient doctrine which all the ancients— Indians, Persians, Greeks and Romans—record in their individual histories. Celsus' point in this opening section is to show the unity of belief, history, and custom which the Christians, as apostates from Judaism and "the Mosaic history," violate. It can be said that Celsus' syncretistic tendencies are most in evidence in his opening sallies. He shows no great love of Judaism (which he finds a pla- giarizing religion), and even less for the strict monotheism of Moses, whom he considers a sorcerer. "It matters not a bit," he argues, "what one calls the supreme god—or whether one uses Greek names or Indian names or the names formerly used by the Egyptians."

Celsus' real venom is reserved for the Christians, who have inherited the worst features of Judaism—namely its

radical monotheism and exclusivism—and add to these
the worship of a man thought to be a son of God yet by all
accounts unworthy of such a title. His attack on the gospel
version of the life of Jesus is a masterpiece of diatribe, put
together, it would seem, from bits of polemical traditions
circulating amongst Jewish and pagan writers: hence, the
story of Jesus' illegitimacy,[78] the legend that he was the
son of a Roman soldier, and that he learned magic spells in
Egypt. All of these are paralleled in Jewish lore and go
back to early prototypes.[79] In dealing with Christian
sources, chiefly with the gospel of Matthew and arguably
with Marcionite and gnostic gospels as well, Celsus acts
the rationalist, pointing up inconsistencies, absurdities,
and analogues with the delight of a prosecuting attorney:
Who witnessed the apotheosis of Jesus in the Jordan? Why
should it be thought that the Old Testament prophecies
speak of Jesus only, when they could as easily be applied
to a thousand others? Why, if Jesus was indeed God's
beloved son, did God not help him out of his calamity but
rather leave him to die like a beggar? In certain places,
Celsus' attack is directed at unsatisfying or incomplete aspects of the story, as for example his discussion of Matthew 2.16, Herod's slaughter of the newborns: "If Herod
did this in order to prevent you from becoming king when
you were grown up instead of him, why then did you not
become king?" In other instances, the attack centers on
Jesus' character or on the credulity and unsavoriness of his
disciples. If he was a god, "Why was he not eager to make
public anything he professed to do?" If his divinity was
evident to his followers, "Why was he betrayed by those
closest to him?"

For Celsus, such inconsistencies are fatal. Even Jesus'
behavior is not becoming of a god: he was a sorcerer; he
flinched in the face of adversity; he was disrespectful of
the customs of his people; one even hears of his eating
habits: "Does the body of a god need nourishment?"

Celsus shows remarkable insight into the apologetic character of the gospel writings. Unlike modern readers who know the gospels chiefly as the canonical documents of the Christian church, Celsus knew them as missionary literature—as propaganda and proclamation—rather than as sacred biography. In this respect Celsus was the first of the New Testament demythologizers, a title he shares in the history of the church with Porphyry, Voltaire, Tom Paine, D. F. Strauss, Arthur Drews, and Rudolf Bultmann. "Let us not omit this: The writings of the disciples contain only those facts about Jesus that put a flattering face on the events of his life." And again, "Your fables have not been well enough constructed to conceal this monstrous fiction: I have heard that some of your interpreters . . . are on the inconsistencies and, pen in hand, alter the original writings three, four, and several more times over in order to be able to deny the contradictions in the face of criticism." Central to his argument was the notion that Jesus' death had been unplanned and unforeseen, and that the gospel writers make an unconvincing effort to conceal what, on its face, is the fundamental embarrassment of Christianity: "You admit that Jesus suffered and died, rather than saying, as you might, that he appeared to endure suffering. Yet what evidence do you point to to suggest that he anticipated this suffering? And if he was at some point a dead man, how can he have been immortal?" In Celsus' view, Jesus could only have been a god if his triumph over death had been transacted at the time of the crucifixion. The very fact that the resurrection—unlike the crucifixion—was an event not witnessed by the Jews casts doubt on the story propagated by the Christians, who might be expected to say that their master performed such a feat. More to the point, the Christians seem unaware that "multitudes have invented similar tales to lead simpleminded hearers astray," Zamolxis, Pythagoras, Orpheus, and Herakles being only the most famous examples. Here it would seem

Celsus' "epicurean" tendencies stand out in boldest relief: for while he demands proof, in the form of witnesses, for the Christian story, his argument centers on the "question of resurrection from the body as a possibility given to mortals." His challenge is based on the belief that the Christian account, like all other such accounts, is purely legendary.

• Celsus interrupts his dialogue between a Jew and a Christian to enter into a discussion of the movement itself. From this section of his work we learn that he is well aware of the internal divisions of the church, a situation otherwise known from the writings of the church fathers.[80] According to Celsus the Christians of the earliest period were unified in purpose, but more recently they have broken out into various divisions and parties, "so that today they have in common only one thing: the name Christian." Although silent about the immorality alleged of the cult by earlier writers, Celsus is highly suspicious of the tactics used by the Christians in their attempts to persuade others of their beliefs, being convinced that their rituals are designed to excite the congregations and to cloud the reason. He compares Christian celebrations to the phrenetic liturgies of the cult of Cybele, and their effects to the hypnotic trances induced by Egyptian priests. While outwardly iconoclastic, the Christians nonetheless "worship a man who was arrested and died," and such worship cannot be accounted better than that of pagans. It is at this point that Celsus launches into his most violent attack upon the Christians themselves: "By the fact that they themselves admit that (only the ignorant and uneducated) are worthy of their God they show that they want and are able to convince only the foolish, dishonorable and stupid, and only slaves, women and little children." Christian teachers exploit the young and the intellectually weak and boast that they have come to appeal to the unrighteous, thus pitching their message to people who by their own admission are unworthy of salvation.

In the Christian God's preference for the unvirtuous, Celsus sees not goodness but malefaction: a god who can be moved by feelings of compassion is a god who sanctions evil. As a philosopher, he shares Galen's (and Plato's) belief that the end of philosophy is moral action; Christianity excoriates learning as a means to virtue and seems to say that God prefers sinners to those who have learned the way of virtue. Such a god "can be influenced by the odd tear or display of emotion." Perhaps, he reasons, a good man would be of no use to such a god, since such a god proves himself chiefly in his exercise of mercy. No wonder, therefore, they preach against the philosophers as they do: "Knowledge is a disease for the soul and the soul that acquires knowledge will perish."

Celsus detects, however, a fundamental inconsistency in the Christian God. A truly good god would be able to save men by his divine power alone and thus prove himself omnipotent. Why should it be necessary for such a god to resort to trivial measures—to descend from the heights; what could be the motive for such a descent? If to make himself known, then clearly his purpose remained unfulfilled, given the inconspicuousness of Jesus' life and influence. Celsus' critique here centers on the contradiction between the purpose and mode of revelation, and the bearing of this contradiction on the Christian doctrine of God. Rather than all-knowing, he is proved to be unknowing, else he must have foreseen the consequences of his actions; rather than all-powerful, he is proved to be limited, since he seemed unable to prevent the tragedies that befell his son. In line with Marcion's criticism of the demiurge, Celsus characterizes the Christian God as a "wealthy man, just come into some money, who decides to flaunt it in front of his friends. . . . It is petulance and the ambition for power that seems to determine the actions of the Christian

God." Celsus offers, further, that a god who waited so long before helping mankind out of his misery cannot be accounted good: "He watches with indifference as wickedness triumphs over good."

After sallies of a primarily rhetorical sort against the Christian interpretation of the Bible, Celsus turns to consider the two problems he sees as being at the center of the disagreement: the existence and increase of evil, and the doctrine of creation. As to the first, Celsus argues that evil is inherent in matter, and while constant and cyclical in occurrence, cannot by its nature increase. What is incorruptible—namely the soul of man—is made by gods and is hence not susceptible of corruption. In articulating the Plotinian view of evil (*Enneads*, 1.8.9) Celsus challenges the Christian belief that creation, while good *ab origine* in virtue of its divine source, was in a state of entropy until the coming of Jesus as savior of the world. If the amount of evil in the world is constant, then "God can have no need of what the Christians call a new creation" (cf. Isa. 65.17). Echoing Marcion's indictment of the creator, Celsus asks whether the Christian God is no better than "an unskilled laborer who is incapable of building something properly first time around." In the end, the Christians' doctrine of creation is the downfall of their theological system: it is a doctrine marred not only by philosophical naivete, but pocked by human arrogance. The Christians, Celsus complains, inherit from the Jews the notion that the world was made solely for the benefit of mankind. When it does not conspicuously serve this purpose, they immediately call for a new order that suits them, ascribing their failures to an increase in evil ordained by their god. Such a belief is responsible for the Christian doctrine of redemption, which centers on the mistaken idea that God abandons his creation for long periods of time, and then after a period of neglect decides to return it to a better state.

This fickleness on the part of the creator leads Celsus to

conclude that the Christian God is contradictory in the purposes he has established for his creatures: having failed to make a perfect world, he then punishes humanity for his failures—or at least those who do not profess the Christian faith. "It is equally silly of these Christians to suppose that when their god applies the fire (like a common cook!) all the rest of mankind will be thoroughly roasted and that they alone will escape unscorched—not just those alive at the time, mind you, but (they say) those long since dead will rise up from the earth possessing the same bodies as they did before." Celsus' premises in this section can be summarized as follows:

a. The Christian God is not all-powerful, else he would have been able to bring creation into line with his purposes.

b. The existence of a willful and disobedient creation that operates contrary to the will of the creator suggests that he is not good; he is ready to reward those who do his will, but is constrained to punish those who do not.

c. Finally, the Christian God proves his inferiority to the impassible first principle of Greek speculation in decreeing the resurrection of the flesh, a doctrine he regards as "both nauseating and impossible."

It can be said that for Celsus, the Christian formulation of the afterlife, stressing as it did the physical survival of the body, is the most unreasonable part of their teaching, both because it violates the Platonic ideal of immortality as a state of being unencumbered by the impermanence of matter, and because it attributes an intention to God which, by his nature, he cannot possess.

• Celsus follows with an attack on the unoriginality of Christian teaching and conflicts within the Christian movement at large. Here he shows knowledge of a variety of gnostic and rigorist movements, including several, of special interest, that trace their foundation to women apostles. Thus he knows of Christian sects named for Helen of Samaria, the legendary consort of Simon Magus; of others named for Marcellina, Salome, Mariamne (= Miriam, the mother of Jesus?), and for Martha, the sister of Lazarus (John 11.1f.). The polemical point of cataloguing these groups notwithstanding, one cannot but be impressed by the number of women-founded sects known to Celsus; nor is there good reason to doubt the accuracy of his list, since Irenaeus too reports the existence of Egyptian sectaries devoted to Marcellina, a follower of Carpocrates,[81] and Hipploytus comments (with what degree of accuracy it is difficult to determine) on the prominence of Miriamne among the Ophites.[82] Salome and Martha figure in the gnostic tract known as the *Pistis Sophia*,[83] and according to Clement,[84] Salome—whose prestige was already guaranteed in the resurrection tradition preserved in Mark's gospel (16.1)—was prominent in the *Gospel of the Egyptians*. As an observer of the young religion, Celsus could not but be struck by the divisions in the church and the resultant failure of the Christians to produce a univocal doctrine of God. This leads him in turn to a highly discursive, even carping treatment of gnostic Christianity and the ditheism of the Marcionites. For Celsus, however, the postulation of two gods—one the creator, the other a savior—is merely a materialization of the dichotomy which the orthodox are themselves unable to resolve without compromising the doctrine of the supreme God's immutability: either the one God changes his mind arbitrarily, now threatening and condemning, now forgiving and redeeming, or else the world is divided, as the Persians had long before maintained, between gods whose purposes are hostile.

• Even allowing for Origen's manipulation of his source, the remainder of Celsus' polemic is repetitious and facile.

The unworthiness of the Christian God, the absurdity of the incarnation, and the silliness of those who hold to the new religion are once again dredged up for ridicule. To this Celsus adds a short digression on the unoriginality of Christian ethics and a plea for the use of reason in the determination of religious precepts. The Christians, he asserts, are not the only ones who abhor violence and disdain the use of force as a response to injury; nor are they the only ones who refuse the worship of images. He repeats as well his contempt for those who worship as a god "a man who appeared only recently" and who require every reference to God to include some reference to Jesus—doubtless a comment targeted at the Christian practice of praying in the name of Jesus: "When they call him a son of God, they are not really paying homage to God; rather, they are attempting to exalt Jesus to the heights."

Perhaps in the last analysis it is precisely this aspect of Christian belief that most exercises Celsus; for if the Christians are ready to pay homage to one son of God, then why not to those officially declared sons of God by legitimate authority? That the Christians had long since sacrificed the monotheism of their spiritual fathers is assumed; their offense, so it seems to the pagan eye, is in "trying to ensure (through an iconoclasm directed at the recognized gods) that Jesus would be preserved as god and lord of the cult, unrivaled by any other." In so doing, however, they inadvertantly acknowledge the existence of other gods; and it follows for Celsus that if such gods exist, they must exist at the pleasure of the supreme God and are hence worthy of honor—even from the Christians.

The charge of exclusivity and religious clannishness pervades the closing section of Celsus' diatribe. The portrait he paints is of a salvation cult drunk on its own success in making converts; Christian teachers who deal in magic and healing for the entertainment of the crowd, enthusiasts of various stripes who, certain of their possession of the spirit, curse statues of Zeus and Apollo, then boast that they are protected against reprisal by virtue of their god's superior power. Confronted with somber social realities—the fact that they are liable to punishment and death for their actions—the Christians counter that, as nothing happens contrary to God's will, even their punishment must work for his glorification and toward the eventual triumph of his kingdom. Were one to view Celsus' riposte to the Christians only in terms of the manifest destiny which second-century martyrs already decreed for the movement, then his ridicule would certainly seem unenlightened. In its own time, however, Celsus' voice is the voice of the establishment and tradition. The Christians are dangerous precisely because they put the advancement of their beliefs above the common good and the welfare of the state.

THE TEXT

The Greek text of Origen's *Against Celsus* upon which the present translation is based is Koetschau's edition of the Vatican manuscript ("A," Vat. gr. 386. thirteenth century, in *Die griechischen christlichen Schriftsteller* 2–3 [Berlin, 1899]). The attempted reconstructions of the *Alēthēs Logos* by Bader (1940), Otto Glöckner (1924), and Theodor Keim (1873) have been consulted, but no attempt has been made to restore the original order of Celsus' work. It is now widely recognized that Origen abbreviates and omits passages of his opponent's book with some regularity (see, e.g., *Contra Celsum* 2.32, 2.79; 6.22; 6.26; 3.64; 6.17, 50, 74; 7.27, 32). This recognition notwithstanding, a majority of scholars would put the percentage of Celsus' work accessi-

ble through Origen's response at around 70 percent (thus
K. J. Neumann, J. Quasten et al.).

Reference has been made throughout to the magisterial
English translation of the *Contra Celsum* by Professor Henry Chadwick and to the 1712 translation of James Bellamy.

NOTES

N.B. Consult the "List of Ancient Works Cited" on pp. xi–xiii for full titles abbreviated in this section.

1. A discussion of the anti-heretical features of the New Testament canon, with special reference to the influence of Marcionism, can be found in John Knox, *Marcion and the New Testament: An Essay on the Early History of the Canon* (London, 1950).

2. Matt. 3.7–10; Luke 3.7–9: a saying of John the Baptist common to the source underlying the gospels of Matthew and Luke.

3. Matt. 4.17; cf. Mark 13.29–31. The ground-breaking discussion of Jesus' eschatological outlook is to be found in Albert Schweitzer, *The Quest of the Historical Jesus* (London, 1910), originally published as *Von Reimarus zu Wrede*, 1906).

4. See note 1 above.

5. The religious context of the Christian eucharist is provided by a variety of mystery religions and particularly by the celebrations connected with the cult of Mithras. See Richard Reitzenstein, *The Hellenistic Mystery Religions: Their Basic Ideas and Significance* (Pittsburgh, Pa., 1978), esp. pp. 11–89.

6. Martin Werner, *The Formation of Christian Dogma*, (London, 1957), p. 25.

7. Cf. Wisdom of Solomon 10.3; Jubilees 4.1–5; Apocalypse of Moses 3.2; Testaments of the Twelve Patriarchs.

8. Ignatius of Antioch, *Epistle to the Ephesians*, 20.2; *Epistle to the Romans*, 7.3.

9. Justin Martyr, *First Apology*, 66.

10. *Epistles*, 10.96; Trajan's reply, *Epistles*, 10.97 (in R. A. B. Mynors, eds., Oxford Classical Texts, 1963).

11. Clement of Alexandria, *Miscellanies*, 3.2.10.

12. Fronto, quoted by Minucius Felix in the *Octavius*, 9.5–6; in Ancient Christian Writers, 39, ed. G. W. Clarke (New York, 1974).

13. *Octavius* 9.5–6.
14. Epiphanius of Salamis, *Panarion*, 26.4–5.
15. Justin, 1 *Apology*, 7.
16. Tertullian of Carthage, *A Prescription against the Heretics*, 43.
17. Tertullian, *To the Nations*, 7, 8; *Apology*, 11.
18. Tertullian, *Apology*, 39.
19. Tertullian, *Apology*, 39.
20. Tertullian, *Apology*, 50.
21. Tertullian, *Apology*, 9.
22. Tertullian, *Apology*, 35.
23. Tertullian, *To the Nations*, 15.
24. Tertullian, *To the Nations*, 14.
25. Tertullian, *Apology*, 45.
26. Clement of Alexandria, *Exhortation to the Greeks*, 2; in G. W. Butterworth's edition (London, 1919).
27. Clement of Alexandria, *Exhortation*, 2.
28. Clement of Alexandria, *Exhortation*, 2.
29. Clement of Alexandria, *Exhortation*, 2.
30. Tertullian, *To the Nations*, 15.
31. Justin, *First Apology*, 54.
32. Joshua ben Pandera is execrated in certain midrashim as a heretic who "lived a life of deceit" and "caused Israel to go astray" through his apostasy. See R. T. Herford, *Christianity in Talmud and Midrash* (New York, 1903); Joseph Klausner, *Jesus of Nazareth* (London, 1925); and R. J. Hoffmann, *Jesus, Outside the Gospels* (Buffalo, 1984), pp. 37–53.
33. Lucian, *The Death of Peregrinus*, 10–13; in Lionel Casson, ed., *Selected Satires of Lucian* (New York, 1962).
34. Lucian, *Peregrinus*, 10–13.
35. Lucian, *Peregrinus*, 13–15.
36. *Against Celsus*, 1.9.
37. Eusebius of Caesarea, *Ecclesiatical History*, 5.13.5.
38. Suetonius, *Lives of the Caesars*, 5.16 (Nero).
39. Epictetus, *Dissertations*, 4.6.7.
40. Marcus Aurelius, *Meditations*, 11.3.
41. For a general discussion of Galen's views, see Richard Walzer, *Galen on Jews and Christians* (London, 1949).
42. Galen, cited from fragments given in Walzer, 48–49.
43. In the case of Porphyry, the reader is referred to Adolf von Harnack, *Porphyrius, "Gegen die Christen"* (Berlin, 1916). According to Harnack, Porphyry was the pagan philosopher cited by Macarius Magnes (early fifth century) in the *Apocriticus* (English trans. by T. W. Crafer [New York, 1919], esp. pp. 51–161).

44. On the thematic development of pagan anti-Christian polemic, see the essays in *The Conflict Between Paganism and Christianity*, ed. Arnaldo Momigliano (Oxford, 1963).

45. Theodor Keim, *Celsus' Wahres Wort* (Zurich, 1873); cf. Pierre Labriolle, *La Réaction païenne: étude sur la polémique antichrétienne* (Paris, 1934). The standard contemporary discussion is that of Pierre Nautin, *Origène, sa vie et son oeuvre* (Paris, 1977).

46. Cf. Eusebius, *Ecclesiatical History*, 6.36.2.

47. Origen, *Against Celsus*, Preface, 4.

48. Galen, *On the Appropriate Books*, 16.

49. Lucian, *Alexander, The False Prophet*, 38–39.

50. Lucian, *Alexander*, 21; cf. 25, 43, 61.

51. In *Origen, Contra Celsum* (Cambridge, 1953), Introduction, p. xxv.

52. Origen, *Against Celsus*, praef., 4.

53. Origen, *Against Celsus*, 1.68.

54. Origen, *Against Celsus*, 1.8.

55. Keim, *Celsus' Wahres Wort*, pp. 275–93.

56. Robert Wilken, *The Christians as the Romans Saw Them* (New Haven, Conn., 1984), p. 95.

57. Tertullian, *Against Marcion*, 5.19.7.

58. Cf. Origen, *Against Celsus*, 1.10.

59. Lucian, *Alexander*, 61.

60. Lucian, *Alexander*, 21.

61. Origen, *Against Celsus*, 1.6.

62. Cf. Origen, *Against Celsus*, 1.9; Lucian, *Peregrinus*, 13f.; *Alexander*, 38.

63. See Origen's comments, *Against Celsus*, 8.69; 8.71, and Chadwick's discussion, *Contra Celsum*, xxvi.

64. Theodor Keim, *Celsus' Wahres Wort*, 271.

65. Philip Schaff, *History of the Christian Church*. Vol. 2: *Ante-Nicene Christianity* (Grand Rapids, Mich., 1910), p. 90.

66. Schaff, *History*, p. 90.

67. Schaff, *History*, p. 90.

68. Wilken, *The Christians*, p. 117.

69. Origen, *Against Celsus*, 5.26.

70. Wilken, *The Christians*, p. 124.

71. Tertullian, *Apology*, 35.

72. Tertullian, *To the Nations*, 8.

73. Tertullian, *Apology*, 35.

74. Tertullian, *Apology*, 32.

75. Tertullian, *Apology*, 37.

76. Tertullian, *To the Nations*, 8.

77. Origen, *Against Celsus*, 8.69.

78. See the discussion in Hoffmann, *Jesus, Outside the Gospels*, pp. 39–43.

79. Examples in David Cartlidge and David L. Dungan, *Documents for the Study of the Gospels* (Philadelphia, 1980), pp. 129–80.

80. See for example Justin, 1 *Apology*, 7. Justin defends such differentiation on the grounds that Christianity is a philosophy; he opposes heresy at the same time in arguing that not all philosophies are "true."

81. Irenaeus, *Against the Heresies*, 1.25.6.

82. The sect may be the same as the Naasenes, actually a group of gnostic sects whose name derives from the Greek term for "serpent" (*ophis*) and who seem to have attributed special significance to the serpent as the representative of a higher god. Hippolytus mentions the Ophites (*Refutation of Heresies*, 5.7.1) together with Peratae and the Sethians; Irenaeus lists them (*Against the Heresies*, 1.30) with the Cainites. See also, R. M. Grant, *Gnosticism: An Anthology* (1961), pp. 52–59.

83. Cf. *The First Apocalypse of James*, V.3, 40.26.

84. Clement of Alexandria, *Miscellanies*, 3.45.63.

On the True Doctrine

I. INTRODUCTION

The cult of Christ is a secret society whose members huddle together in corners for fear of being brought to trial and punishment.[1] Their persistence is the persistence of a group threatened by a common danger, and danger is a more powerful incentive to fraternal feeling than is any oath. As to their doctrine, it was originally barbarian, and while even barbarians are capable of discovering truth, it happens to be the case that Greeks are best equipped to judge the merit of what passes for truth these days. They also practice their rites in secret in order to avoid the sentence of death that looms over them. There is nothing new or impressive about their ethical teaching; indeed, when one compares it to other philosophies, their simplemindedness becomes apparent. Take their aversion to what they term idolatry. As Herodotus shows, the Persians long before our time held the view that things made with human hands cannot be regarded as gods. Indeed, it is preposterous that the work of a craftsman (often the worst sort of person!) should be considered a god. The wise Heracleitus says that "those who worship images as gods are as foolish as men who talk to the walls."[2]

The Christians claim to get some sort of power from pronouncing the names of demons or saying certain incantations, always incorporating the name Jesus and a short story about him in the formula.[3] Even this practice is old stuff: Jesus himself was thought to work wonders by the use of magic and incantations. He knew that others would follow him in these practices, yet he seems to have expelled those who did from his society. Perhaps this is the origin of the hypocrisy for which the Christians are so

53

well known: Was he right to drive them away for copying him?[4] Being guilty of magic himself he had no reason to accuse others, nor could they be accounted bad men for following their leader.

More and more the myths put about by these Christians are better known than the doctrines of the philosophers. Who has not heard the fable of Jesus' birth from a virgin or the stories of his crucifixion and resurrection? And for these fables the Christians are ready to die—indeed do die. Now I would not want to say that a man who got into trouble because of some eccentric belief should have to renounce his belief or pretend that he has renounced it. But the point is this, and the Christians would do well to heed it: One ought first to follow reason as a guide before accepting any belief, since anyone who believes without testing a doctrine is certain to be deceived. We have plenty of examples in our own time: the snivelling beggars of Cybele, the soothsayers, the worshippers of Mithras and Sabazius; those gullible believers in the apparitions of Hecate, and assorted other gods.[5] Just as the charlatans of the cults take advantage of a simpleton's lack of education to lead him around by the nose, so too with the Christian teachers: they do not want to give or to receive reasons for what they believe. Their favorite expressions are "Do not ask questions, just believe!" and: "Your faith will save you!" "The wisdom of this world," they say, "is evil; to be simple is to be good."[6] If only they would undertake to answer my question—which I do not ask as one who is trying to understand their beliefs (there being little to understand!) But they refuse to answer, and indeed discourage asking questions of any sort. For this reason I have undertaken to compose a treatise for their edification, so that they can see for themselves the true character of the doctrines they have chosen to embrace and the true sources of their opinions.

II. THE UNORIGINALITY OF
THE CHRISTIAN FAITH

Many of the nations of the world hold doctrines similar to those espoused by the Christians. This leads some thinkers to conclude that there is an original source for the various opinions that purport to be the "true" [religious] doctrine. The historians of the various nations have given us their accounts—accounts, it goes without saying, that offer us a very one-sided version of their national religion and a biased view of the religions of surrounding peoples. The prophets of the Jews and their great hero, Moses, wrote the history of their people in a way designed to favor their beliefs. The Egyptian view of the Jews, not surprisingly, is quite different. Yet behind these views, these national prejudices, is an ancient doctrine that has existed from the beginning—a doctrine, so it is said, maintained by the wisest men of all nations and cities. This doctrine has been held not only by the sages among the Jews, but by the wise men of the Egyptians, the Assyrians, the Indians, Persians, Odrysians, Samothracians, and Eleusinians. The Galactophagi of Homer, the Druids of Gaul, and even the Getae (for example) believe doctrines very close to those believed by the Jews—indeed, before the Jews. Linus, Musaeus, Orpheus, Pherecydes, Zoroaster the Persian, and Pythagoras understood these doctrines, and their opinions were recorded in books which are still to be consulted.[7]

The Mosaic history is one among many, and those who attempt to universalize it or to disguise its partiality by treating the books of Moses allegorically [wiser though they may be than those who take such accounts at face value] are being led astray and deceived.

Were we to read the literature of but one nation, we would conclude that there had been but one flood, one conflagration, one disruption of the created order. But in reality there have been many floods, many conflagrations—those floods in the time of Deucalion and the fire in the time of Phaeton being more recent than the rest.[8]

The Greeks of course thought these upheavals ancient since they did not possess records of earlier events, such records being destroyed in the course of floods and conflagrations. Moses heard of such beliefs, beliefs current among the wise nations and among distinguished men, and thus received for himself a certain reputation for having divine powers. These doctrines he used in order to educate the Jews. Yet none of what he taught can be considered original: the rite of circumcision, for example—which I do not criticize—came to the Jews from Egypt where the rite is used to produce magical effects.[9] Yet without rational cause, the goatherds and shepherds followed Moses, who taught them that there was but one God—deluded, apparently, by his rather naive beliefs—and caused them to forsake their natural inclinations to credit the existence of the gods. For our part, we acknowledge the many: Mnemosyne, who gave birth to the Muses by Zeus; Themis, Mother of the Hours; and so on. Yet these goatherds and shepherds came to believe in one god and called him the Most High—Adonai, the Heavenly One—or sometimes Sabaoth, or whatsoever—and came to discredit all other gods. Yet in excluding the other names of the highest god, have not they shown their foolishness! It matters not a bit what one calls the supreme God—or whether one uses Greek names or Indian names or the names used formerly by the Egyptians. Further, for all their exclusiveness about the highest god, do not the Jews also worship angels, and are they not addicted to sorcery, as indeed their scripture shows Moses himself was?[10]

I shall take up the matter of the Jewish doctrines in due course. First, however, I must deal with the matter of

Jesus, the so-called savior, who not long ago taught new doctrines and was thought to be a son of God. This savior, I shall attempt to show, deceived many and caused them to accept a form of belief harmful to the wellbeing of mankind. Taking its root in the lower classes, the religion continues to spread among the vulgar: nay, one can even say it spreads because of its vulgarity and the illiteracy of its adherents.[11] And while there are a few moderate, reasonable, and intelligent people who are inclined to interpret its beliefs allegorically,[12] yet it thrives in its purer form among the ignorant.

Let us imagine what a Jew—let alone a philosopher—might put to Jesus: "Is it not true, good sir, that you fabricated the story of your birth from a virgin to quiet rumours about the true and unsavory circumstances of your origins? Is it not the case that far from being born in royal David's city of Bethlehem, you were born in a poor country town, and of a woman who earned her living by spinning?[13] Is it not the case that when her deceit was discovered, to wit, that she was pregnant by a Roman soldier named Panthera[14] she was driven away by her husband—the carpenter—and convicted of adultery? Indeed, is it not so that in her disgrace, wandering far from home, she gave birth to a male child in silence and humiliation? What more? Is it not so that you hired yourself out as a workman in Egypt, learned magical crafts, and gained something of a name for yourself which now you flaunt among your kinsmen?"[15]

What absurdity! Clearly the Christians have used the myths of the Danae and the Melanippe, or of the Auge and the Antiope in fabricating the story of Jesus' virgin birth.[16] A beautiful woman must his mother have been, that this Most High God should want to have intercourse with her! An interesting point in itself, since if, as their philosophers (copying ours) say, God by nature does not love corruptible bodies, he cannot love a woman. Are we

to think that this high God would have fallen in love with
a woman of no breeding—one unknown and unregarded
even by her neighbors? Odd that the kingdom of God, the
core of their teaching, is made to hang on the disgrace of a
rejected woman, whose husband turned her aside. Let us
pursue further the questions put to this Jesus by the Jew:
"When you were bathing in the Jordan near John, I understand you saw what looked like a bird fly towards you out
of the air.[17] Now let me understand what witnesses saw
this wondrous event. And I should be most eager to know
who heard the voice attesting that you are the Son of God?
For I have so far heard only your voice, and have but your
word for it. Now perhaps you will want to argue that we
have the words of the holy prophets—that they bore witness concerning you. With due respect, I must ask why
you are to be taken as the subject of these prophecies
rather than the thousands of others who lived after the
prophecy was uttered? What can be applied to you surely
can be applied to others; you are not the only one who
goes about begging and claiming to be the Son of God.
And would it not seem reasonable that if you are, as you
say, God's son, God would have helped you out of your
calamity, or that you would have been able to help yourself? You say as well that divine grace makes everyone a
son of God.[18] This being so, what is the difference between you and anyone else?

"But let us review a story about your birth: You say that
Chaldeans came to worship you as God while you were
still an infant,[19] and that they told Herod the Tetrarch of
this, and that he sent men to kill those born just at that
time, hoping to destroy you along with them. This was
done, so it is said, in order to ensure that you would not
reign as king when you were grown up. Now this is very
puzzling: if Herod did this in order to prevent you from
becoming king when you were grown instead of him, why
then have you not become a king? Why—though a son of

God—do you go about begging for food, cowering before the threats of the people, and wandering about homeless?"

According to the Jews, Jesus collected around him ten or eleven[20] unsavory characters—tax collectors, sailors, and the like, and these scurried about making a living as best they were able, usually through double dealing and in otherwise questionable ways. But (the Jew will want to say): "Is it not wonderful that you survived at all! I mean, what when you were an infant you had to be taken away to Egypt lest you should be murdered. I am disturbed by the news that you, though a god, should have been afraid of death. An angel from heaven persuaded your family of the danger that you were doomed lest they escape with you.[21] This is the second angel, if I hear rightly, who had been sent to provide a warning. One wonders why many more could not have been sent by the great God above—you being his beloved son! After all, the old myths of the Greeks that attribute a divine birth to Perseus, Amphion, Aeacus and Minos are equally good evidence of their wondrous works on behalf of mankind—and are certainly no less lacking in plausibility than the stories of your followers. What have you done by word or deed that is quite so wonderful as those heroes of old? Challenged in the Temple to produce some sign that you were the son of God[22] you showed us nothing.

"Perhaps you will point to those tricks about which your disciples boast: those cures and resurrections, or feeding the crowds with but a few loaves (and having some left over to boot!).[23] Monstrous tales, to be sure. But let us say for the sake of argument that such things were actually done by you. Are they then so different from the sort of things done by sorcerers—who also claim to do wonderful miracles, having been taught their tricks by the Egyptians. The sorcerers at least, for a few pence, make their magic available to everyone in the marketplace. They drive away demons, conquer diseases of all kinds, and make the dead heroes of the past appear—indeed sitting at long tables and eating imaginary cakes and dishes. They make things move about, as if they were alive—all illusion to be sure, but quite appealing to the average imagination. Now I ask you: As these men are able to do such wonderful things, ought we not regard them also as sons of God? Or ought we rather to say that they are the contrivances of evil men who are themselves possessed by demons?[24] I think, Jesus, that the High God would not have chosen a body such as yours; nor would the body of a god have been born as you were born. We even hear of your eating habits. What! Does the body of a god need such nourishment? And we hear often of your unsuccessful attempts to win over others to your cause—the tricks evidently not being enough to hold their attention. One wonders why a god should need to resort to your kind of persuasion— even eating a fish after your resurrection.[25] I should rather think that your actions are those of one hated by God, the actions of a sorcerer." So says our Jew to Jesus.

III. ADDRESS TO THE JEWS

I now address myself to those Jewish believers who have turned aside from the faith of their fathers, deluded and ludicrously misled by this Jesus, and become strangers to their heritage. Says our Jew to them: "Why have you, O citizens of Israel, left the law of our fathers and become slaves to the power of this man whom we were just before addressing? You have been deceived. You have deserted Israel for another name. When we punished this Jesus who deceived you,[26] you abandoned the law—or would you rather say that you take your start from the law of the fathers? But why take your start in the religion of the Jews? How can you despise the origins in which you yourselves claim to be rooted? Or can you name some other origin for your doctrine than our law? Is it not true that our own prophets speak of God among men. John, whom you revere as a prophet, was himself a Jew. And as for the doctrine central to your belief—the belief that the dead are raised and that God will dispense judgment to the righteous and to the unrighteous, your religion teaches nothing new.

"Let us look at your Messiah. Jesus, according to your writings, kept all the Jewish festivals and customs. He even took part in our sacrifices.[27] Is this the hallmark of the Son of God? This god of yours is arrogant. He told great lies. He was a blasphemer and a profaner of the Sabbath. Worst of all, he managed to convince you to follow him in his profanity and lying, or those of you who appeared ready to be deceived. He is a liar, because while respecting on occasion the outward forms of our observances, yet he did not hesitate to abandon them for the sake of convenience: circumcision, the feasts of new moons, the distinction between what is clean and what unclean. All of this was done for the deceitful purpose of winning over the Jews, only thereafter to lead them astray. The one who will punish the unrighteous will come from God, and on that day, how you will despise this Jesus!

"Look at your god: How can you regard him as a god when as a matter of fact he was not eager to make public anything he professed to do?[28] After he had been tried and condemned and it had been decided that he should be punished, where did we find him? Hiding—trying to escape.[29] And was he not even betrayed by those whom he was silly enough to call disciples?[30] If he was a god, is it likely that he would have run away? Would he have permitted himself to be arrested? Most of all: Would a god—a savior, as you say, and son of the Most High God—be betrayed by the very men who had been taught by him and shared everything with him? What an absurdity you have chosen to make a doctrine: no general worth his salt could have broached betrayal by the thousands he led; not even a robber chieftain captaining a crew of brigands would have been handed over by those whom he had tried to lead. But Jesus! He was betrayed by those closest to him, those under his authority, and he ruled neither like a good general, nor (when he had fooled his disciples) did he command the respect of his followers even to such a degree as robbers feel for their chief.

"I could continue along these lines, suggesting a good deal about the affairs of Jesus' life that does not appear in your own records. Indeed, what I know to be the case and what his disciples tell are two very different stories. But let me pass over these details. Let us disregard the treachery of his disciples and the nonsensical idea that Jesus foresaw everything that was to happen to him[31] (an obvious attempt to conceal the humilating facts). But let us not omit this: the writings of the disciples contain only those facts about Jesus that put a flattering face on the events of his life. It is as if someone were saying out of one side of his mouth that a man is righteous, while admitting at the same time that the man is an evildoer; or, put differently, showing a man to be a murderer while saying he is holy; or while saying he is risen, proving him to be dead; and then—above it all—claiming that he predicted it! You admit that Jesus suffered and died (rather than saying, as you might, that he appeared to endure suffering).[32] Yet what evidence do you point to to suggest that he anticipated this suffering? And if he was at some point a dead man, how can he have been immortal? It seems to me that any god or demon—or for that matter, any sensible man—who foreknew what was going to happen to him would try very hard to avoid such a fate. I mean, if he foreknew both the man who was to betray him and the man who was going to deny him, it would seem they would have feared him as God, and knowing what he knew, that the one would not betray him or the other deny him. Of course, as you tell the story, they both betrayed him and denied him without any thought for this at all. If people conspire against a man who anticipates their conspiracy and tells them of it to their face, such traitors commonly turn away from their treachery and are thereafter on their guard. But I conclude that these things did not happen to Jesus because they were foretold. That is quite impossible. No, the very fact that they happened suggests the opposite: namely, that they were wholly unexpected. He had not predicted them. It is impossible to think that those who had already heard of their behavior from Jesus would have carried out their intentions.

"But perhaps," you will argue, "he foretold all these things by virtue of being a god and knowing the hearts and minds of his followers.[33] And what he foreknew must come to pass. If it is thus the case that these things happened according to his divine intention and with his foreknowledge, we must also conclude that Jesus the god led his own disciples and prophets—those with whom he ate and drank—so far astray that they became evil and treacherous. But if he was a god, ought he not rather to have done good to men? Especially to those who followed him? In my book, a man who shared meals with another man would not intend him to betray him, especially if the first was a god! Are we then to say, as your doctrine teaches, that God himself was the conspirator—that God ate with men, only to turn his disciples into traitors and evildoers?

"The things that happened to Jesus were intensely painful. It must have been impossible for him to have prevented them from being so. But if it is true that he foreknew what was to happen—indeed intended it from the start, why is he represented as lamenting and wailing, and supplicating God to make him strong in the face of death. Why does he cry: "Father, if only this cup could pass by me!"[34] A fine God indeed who fears what he is supposed to conquer.

"It is clear to me that the writings of the Christians are a lie, and that your fables have not been well enough constructed to conceal this monstrous fiction. I have even heard that some of your interpreters, as if they had just come out of a tavern, are onto the inconsistencies and, pen in hand, alter the original writings three, four, and several more times over in order to be able to deny the contradictions in the face of criticism."[35]

Let our Jew continue his sally against the Christians, now with a view to the prophets who, so say the Christians, foretold the story of Jesus beforehand: "These same prophecies could easily be applied to a thousand others besides Jesus, for our prophets say that the one who is to come (the Messiah) will be a great prince; he will be the lord of this world, and the leader of nations and armies. From this it is obvious that the prophets do not anticipate a low-grade character like this Jesus—a man who is able to make himself the son of a god by trickery, deceit and the most incredible stories. A true son of God, like the sun that illuminated the world by first illuminating itself, ought first to have been revealed as a true god. The Christians put forth this Jesus not only as the son of God but as the very Logos—not the pure and holy Logos known to the philosophers,[36] mind you, but a new kind of Logos: a man who managed to get himself arrested and executed in the most humiliating of circumstances.

"This boaster and sorcerer whom you designate the Logos is unique in having a human genealogy. The men who fabricated this genealogy were insistent on the point that Jesus was descended from the first man and from the king of the Jews.[37] The poor carpenter's wife seems not to have known she had such a distinguished bunch of ancestors; they were all kept in the closet until such time as they could be of some use. A fine god indeed, this boaster and sorcerer who performed not one godly action, who could not counter even the opposition of men, or avoid the disaster that ended his life in disgrace. According to your tales, the man who sentenced him did not suffer the fate of a Pentheus by going mad[38] or being torn to pieces; rather, Jesus permitted himself to be mocked and bedecked with a purple robe and crowned with thorns. Why did this son of a god not show one glimmer of his divinity under these conditions? Why did he refuse to deliver himself from shame—at least play the man and stand up for his own or for his father's honor? But what does he say when his body is stretched out on the cross? 'Is this blood not ichor such as flows in the veins of the blessed?'[39] When thirsty, he drinks greedily from a sponge full of vinegar and gall, not bearing his thirst with godly patience. Yet you who call yourselves true believers dare to criticize us Jews because we refuse to acknowledge this man as a god or admit that he underwent these sufferings for the good of mankind so that we all may avoid punishment? Have you forgotten that while he lived this Jesus convinced nobody—not even his own disciples—of his divinity, and was punished shamefully for his blasphemies? Were he a god he should not have died, if only in order to convince others for good and all that he was no liar; but die he did—not only that, but died a death that can hardly be accounted an example to men. Nor was he free from blame, as you imagine. Not only was he poor, he was also a coward and a liar as well. Perhaps you Christians will say that having failed to convince men on earth of his divinity, he descended into hell to convince them there. In all of these beliefs you have been deceived; yet you persist doggedly to seek justification for the absurdities you have made doctrines. If the central doctrine of Christianity bears testing, why should we not wonder whether every condemned man is an angel even greater than your divine Jesus? I mean, why not be completely shameless and confess that every robber, every convicted murderer, is neither robber nor murderer but a god? And why? Because he had told his robber band beforehand that he would come to no good end and wind up a dead man. Your case is made the harder because not even his disciples believed in him at the time of his humiliation: those who had heard him preach and were taught by him, when they saw he was heading for trouble, did not stick with him. They were neither willing to die for his sake nor to become martyrs for his cause— they even denied they had known him! Yet on the example of those original traitors, you stake your faith and profess your willingness to die.

"When I ask what arguments you would cite to show that this man was a son of God, you offer that his death was meant to destroy the father of evil.[40] But then, others have been punished by means just as disgraceful. Why did their deaths not bring about an end of evil? Or will you say that he was a son of God because he healed the lame and the blind and (as you declare) raised the dead?"

But—leaving our Jew to ponder for a moment—is this sort of thing not the very essence of sorcery and deception? As the Christians themselves have said, Jesus himself spoke of rivals entering the contest with his followers, wicked men and magicians, who would perform just the same sort of wonders, only under the supervision of Satan.[41] Even Jesus admitted there was nothing exclusively "divine" about working these signs—that they could just as easily be done by wicked men. Nonetheless, in acknowledging this capacity in others, he unwittingly proves his own performances to be a lie. Good Lord! Is it not a silly sort of argument to reckon by the same works that one man is a god whilst his rivals are mere "sorcerers"? Why should we conclude from your argument that the sorcerers are worse than your god—that is if we take the testimony of Jesus about their powers seriously? He himself has said that such works were not produced by any divine nature but were instead the works of cheats and imposters. But to return to our quizzical Jew: Let him ask a question of his countrymen newly converted to the religion of this Jesus:

"Is your belief based on the 'fact' that this Jesus told in advance that he would rise again after his death? That your story includes his predictions of triumphing over the grave? Well, let it be so. Let's assume for the present that he foretold his resurrection. Are you ignorant of the multitudes who have invented similar tales to lead simpleminded hearers astray? It is said that Zamolxis, Pythagoras' servant, convinced the Scythians that he had risen from the dead, having hidden himself away in a cave for several years;[42] and what about Pythagoras himself in Italy![43]—or Rhampsinitus in Egypt.[44] The last of these, by the way, is said to have played dice with Demeter in Hades and to have received a golden napkin as a present from her. Now then, who else: What about Orpheus among the Odrysians,[45] Protesilaus in Thessaly[46] and above all Herakles and Theseus.[47] But quite apart from all these risings from the dead, we must look carefully at the question of the resurrection of the body as a possibility given to mortals. Doubtless you will freely admit that these other stories are legends, even as they appear to me; but you will go on to say that your resurrection story, this climax to your tragedy, is believable and noble. (This, of course, notwithstanding his cry from the cross). I suppose you will say that the earthquake and the darkness that covered the earth at the time of his death prove him a god,[48] and that even though he did not accept the challenge to remove himself from the cross or to escape his persecutors when he was alive, yet he overcame them all by rising from the dead and showing the marks of his punishment, pierced hands and all, to others. But who really saw this? A hysterical woman, as you admit[49] and perhaps one other person—both deluded by his sorcery, or else so wrenched with grief at his failure that they hallu-

cinated him risen from the dead by a sort of wishful thinking. This mistaking a fantasy for reality is not at all uncom-
mon; indeed, it has happened to thousands. Just as possible, these deluded women wanted to impress the others—who had already the good sense to have abandoned
him—by spreading their hallucinations about as "visions." After getting some few to believe them, it was a
small matter for the fire of superstition to spread. If this
Jesus were trying to convince anyone of his powers, then
surely he ought to have appeared first to the Jews who
treated him so badly—and to his accusers—indeed to
everyone, everywhere. Or better, he might have saved
himself the trouble of getting buried and simply have dis-
appeared from the cross. Has there ever been such an
incompetent planner: When he was in the body, he was
disbelieved but preached to everyone; after his resurrection, apparently wanting to establish a strong faith, he
chooses to show himself to one woman and a few com-
rades only. When he was punished, everyone saw; yet
risen from the tomb, almost no one. The Christians are
fond of saying that Jesus wanted to be unnoticed, and
point to places in their sacred books where Jesus enjoins
silence on the demons and those he has healed.[50] But
again, they contradict themselves, condemning the Jews
for failing to recognize the Christ.[51] If he wanted to be
unnoticed, why was the voice from heaven heard, declar-
ing him the Son of God? If he did not want to be unnoticed, then why was he punished and executed? At the
very least it would seem that he would want his followers
to know why he had come to earth. But your Jesus does
not let his followers in on his secret, and thus occasions
their disbelief. This is not my own guessing: I base what I
say on your own writings, which are self-refuting. What
god has ever lived among men who offers disbelief as the
proof of his divinity? What god appears in turn only to
those who already look for his reappearance, and is not

even recognized by them? The sort of god, you should answer, who piles empty abuses on his hearers by threatening them with woes for misunderstanding things which were never made plain to them.[52] What is plain is that this Jesus was a mere man, and rather more a reason to disbelieve in resurrection than to hold fast to the doctrine of our fathers, which says that it is within God's power to raise men from the dead." So our Jew would say to his deceived countrymen.

IV. CHRISTIAN DOCTRINE COMPARED TO THAT OF THE GREEKS

We leave our Jew satisfied to have won his case against the Christians. Returning to consider the truth of their beliefs, I wonder that Christians and Jews argue so foolishly with one another—their contest over whether Jesus was or was not the Messiah reminding me rather of the proverb about the shadow of an ass.[53] In fact, there is really nothing of significance in their dispute: both maintain the quite nonsensical notion that a divine savior was prophesied long ago and would come to dwell among men. All they disagree on is whether he has come or not. The Christians say yes, and cite the miracles of Jesus as proof of his identity. The Jews say that any sorcerer could put forward such proofs, and that the circumstances of Jesus' death prove him an imposter. I am slightly inclined to the latter view myself, since miracles and wonders have indeed occurred everywhere and in all times: Asclepios did mighty works and foretold the futures of cities that kept his cult— Trikka, Epidaurus, Cos, and Pergamum;[54] then there is Aristeas the Proconnesian, or the case of a certain Clazomennian—or of Cleomedes the Astypalean.[55] Yet I am also bound to say that the Jews have a knack of generating such nonsense. By race, they are Egyptian-like folk, and after revolting against their Egyptian cousins and being in turn disinherited by the leaders of Egypt, they struck out on their own, only to experience the same sort of rejection from the Christian cult that arose in their midst. In both instances apostasy bred apostasy, rejection led to rejection.

Now the Christians are just as proud as the Jews. They profess to seek converts, but thrive on martyrdom.[56] I rather suspect that if all men desired to become Christians, the cult would immediately shut the door to converts. At the start of their movement, they were very few in number, and unified in purpose. Since that time, they have spread all around and now number in the thousands. It is not surprising, therefore, that there are divisions among them—factions of all sorts, each wanting to have its own territory. Nor is it surprising that as these divisions have become so numerous, the various parties have taken to condemning each other, so that today they have only one thing—if that—in common: the name "Christian."[57] But despite their clinging proudly to their name, in most other respects they are at odds. I suppose, however, that it is more amazing that there are any points of agreement at all, given the fact their belief rests on no solid foundation. They are agreed, for instance, that outsiders are not to be trusted and that they themselves must remain perpetual apostates from the approved religions.

Now, it will be wondered how men so disparate in their beliefs can persuade others to join their ranks. The Christians use sundry methods of persuasion, and invent a number of terrifying incentives. Above all, they have concocted an absolutely offensive doctrine of everlasting punishment and rewards, exceeding anything the philosophers (who have never denied the punishment of the unrighteous or the reward of the blessed) could have imagined. I have heard that before their ceremonies, where they expand on their misunderstanding of the ancient traditions, they excite their hearers to the point of frenzy with flute music like that heard among the priests of Cybele. In the old religions of Egypt, I recall, a man would be seduced by the magnificence of the shrines—the sacred gardens, the great entrance, the temple surrounded by splendid tents, not to mention the hypnotic effect of the rites themselves, made to be swallowed by the gullible. But once inside, what did the worshiper find? A cat—or a monkey; a dog, crocodile, or goat.[58] The design of the old religion was to impress upon the initiate that he had learned a secret knowledge—that the significance of these animals was given to him and him only. But at least the religion of Egypt transcended the worship of the irrational beasts: the animals were symbols of invisible ideas and not objects of worship in themselves. The religion of the Christians is not directed at an idea but at the crucified Jesus, and this is surely no better than dog or goat worship at its worst.

The Christians ignore the good offices of the Dioscuri, of Herakles, Asclepios, and of Dionysus, and say that these men are not gods because they were humans in the first place. Yet they profess belief in a phantom god who appeared only to members of his little club, and then, so it seems, merely as a kind of ghost. Now in the case of Asclepios, many men, Greeks as well as barbarians, confess that they see him—not a mere phantom, but Asclepios himself, doing his customary good works and foretelling the future.[59] Or take Aristeas, who vanished from men's sight miraculously, then appeared again, and later on visited many parts of the world and recounted his wanderings.[60] Such was his power that even Apollo is said to have commanded the Metapontines to regard Aristeas a god. I hasten to say: nobody any longer believes in Aristeas as a god. So too with Abaris the Hyperborean—who according to Herodotus[61] carried an arrow over the whole world without stopping to eat. Yet even such power did not cause people to make him a god. And the Clazomennian whose soul is said to have left his body from time to time and wandered around on its own.[62] A stupendous wonder indeed—yet no one thinks him a god. And Cleomedes the Astypalean: he got into a chest, shut the lid, and was not to be seen inside when it was broken to bits by those seeking to arrest him.[63] Perhaps he vanished by some act of providence: but it is certain his vanishing did not cause the people to declare him a god.

I emphasize that the Christians worship a man who was arrested and died, after the manner of the Getae who reverence Zamolxis, or those Sicilians who worship Mopsus, the Aracarnanians who worship Amphilochus, or the Thebans who worship Amphiarus and the Lebadians who worship Trophonius.[64] The honor they pay to Jesus is no different from the sort paid to Hadrian's favorite boy, Antinous.[65] Yet they brook no comparison between Jesus and the established gods, such is the effect of the faith that has blurred their judgment. For only a blind faith explains the hold that Jesus has of their imagination. For they stress that he was born a mortal—indeed, that his flesh was as corruptible as gold, silver, and stone. By birth, he shared those carnal weaknesses that the Christians themselves regard as abominable. They will have it, however, that he put aside this flesh in favor of another, and so became a god. But if apotheosis is the hallmark of divinity, why not rather Asclepios, Dionysus, or Herakles, whose stories are far more ancient? I have heard a Christian ridicule those in Crete who show tourists the tomb of Zeus, saying that these Cretans have no reason for doing what they do. It may be so; yet the Christians base their faith on one who rose from a tomb.

Even the more intelligent Christians preach these absurdities. Their injunctions are like this: "Let no one educated, no one wise, no one sensible draw near. For these abilities are thought by us to be evils. But as for anyone ignorant, anyone stupid, anyone uneducated, anyone childish, let him come boldly." By the fact that they themselves admit that these people are worthy of their god, they show that they want and are able to convince only the foolish, dishonorable and stupid, and only slaves, women and little children.

Further, we see that these Christians display their trickery in the marketplace and go around begging. They would not dare to enter into conversation with intelligent men, or to voice their sophisticated beliefs in the presence of the wise. On the other hand, wherever one finds a crowd of adolescent boys, or a bunch of slaves, or a company of fools, there will the Christian teachers be also—showing off their fine new philosophy. In private houses one can see wool workers, cobblers, laundry workers, and the most illiterate country bumpkins, who would not venture to voice their opinions in front of their intellectual betters. But let them get hold of children in private houses—let them find some gullible wives—and you will hear some preposterous statements: You will hear them say, for instance, that they should not pay any attention to their fathers or teachers, but must obey them. They say that their elders and teachers are fools, and are in reality very bad men who like to voice their silly opinions. These Christians claim that they alone know the right way to live, and that if only the children will believe them, they will be happy and their homes will be happy as well. Now if, as they are speaking thus to the children, they happen to see a schoolteacher coming along, some intelligent person, or even the father of one of the children, these Christians flee in all directions, or at least the more cautious of them. The more reckless encourage the children to rebel. They tell the children that they remain silent in the presence of the parents and the schoolteachers only because they do not want to have anything to do with men as corrupt as these pagans, who, did they know what the children had been hearing, would likely punish them for hearing it. These Christians also tell the children that they should leave their fathers and teachers and follow the women and their little chums to the wooldresser's shop, or to the cobbler's or to the washerwoman's shop, so that they might learn how to be perfect. And by this logic they have persuaded many to join them.

Please do not think I criticize the Christians any more bitterly than they deserve. I think anyone may see that the summons to join the other mysteries is rather different, however. It runs: Come forward, whoever has a pure heart and wise tongue, or else, whoever is free of sin and whose soul is pure—you who are righteous and good—come forward.[66] In the mystery religions, such talk is typical, as is the promise that membership brings about a sort of purification from sins. But the call to membership in the cult of Christ is this: Whoever is a sinner, whoever is unwise, whoever is childish—yea, whoever is a wretch—his is the kingdom of God. And so they invite into membership those who by their own account are sinners: the dishonest, thieves, burglars, poisoners, blasphemers of all descriptions, grave robbers.[67] I mean—what other cult actually invites robbers to become members! Their excuse for all of it is that their god was sent to call sinners: well, fair enough. But what about the righteous? How do they account for the fact that their appeal is to the lowest sort of person? Why was their Christ not sent to those who had not sinned—Is it any disgrace not to have sinned? Are they saying that a god who will receive an unrighteous man who repents of his unrighteousness, provided he humbles himself, will *not* receive a righteous man, even if he has remained steadfast in his righteousness and honored God from the beginning of his days?

But of course, the Christians postulate that everyone is a sinner, so that they are able to extend their appeal to the public at large. Now, it is perhaps the case that everyone is inclined to sin—though not everyone does sin. But if it is the case that everyone sins, why did their god not merely call mankind in general to salvation rather than the wicked? I mean, why on earth this preference for sinners?

I suspect I know why the Christians pitch their message as they do: because they are unable to convert anyone truly virtuous and good. This can be the only explanation for their clear preference of the wicked and sinful.

The Christian God is apparently moved by feelings of pity and compassion for the sort of men that hang about the Christian churches, or so at least they believe. Such compassion is a great relief, no doubt, for the evildoer, since he can rely on the fact that even the god who judges his actions is not above being influenced by the odd tear or display of emotion. Do they suggest that a good man would be rejected by such a god? Do they mean to say that the wise are hindered and led astray by their wisdom? Such, at least, I assume to be the case when I consider their vulgar doctrines. I doubt very much that any really intelligent man believes these doctrines of the Christians, for to believe them would require one to ignore the sort of unintelligent and uneducated people who are persuaded by it. And how can one overlook the fact that Christian teachers are only happy with stupid pupils—indeed scout about for the slow-witted.

A teacher of the Christian faith is a charlatan who promises to restore sick bodies to health, but discourages his patients from seeing a first-class physician with a real remedy for fear superior skill and training will show him up.[68] Thus, the Christian teachers warn, "Keep away from physicians." And to the scum that constitutes their assemblies, they say "Make sure none of you ever obtains knowledge, for too much learning is a dangerous thing: knowledge is a disease for the soul, and the soul that acquires knowledge will perish."[69]

Your teacher acts like a drunkard who enters a saloon

and accuses the customers of being drunk—a blind man who preaches to nearsighted men that they have defective eyesight. I bring these accusations against the Christians, and could bring many more (which I refrain from doing); I affirm that they insult God; they lead wicked men astray, offering them all sorts of false hopes and teaching them to hate what is truly good—saying that they should avoid the company of good men.

V. CRITIQUE OF CHRISTIAN TEACHING

I turn now to consider the argument—made by Christians and some Jews—that some god or son of God has come down to the earth as judge of mankind. The Jews say he is still to come (a shameful idea and one really not worth refuting). Now what I should like to know is this: What is God's purpose in undertaking such a descent from the heights? Does he want to know what is going on among men? If he doesn't know, then he does not know everything. If he does know, why does he not simply correct men by his divine power? A fine god indeed who must pay a visit to the regions below, over which he is said to have control. Yet the Christians maintain that he is unable to correct men by divine power without sending someone who is especially adept at saving people from their sins. Furthermore, if God was unknown among men and thus thought himself to be underrated, would he want to make himself known and put those who believed in him to the test along with those who did not, like some wealthy man who has just come into some money and decides to flaunt it among his friends? It is petulance and the ambition for power that seems to determine the actions of the Christian God. Were they consistent, the Christians would argue that a god does not need to be known for his own sake, but rather wishes to give knowledge of himself for salvation—that is to say, in order to make people good and to distinguish the good from those who are bad and deserve punishment. But the Christian God is not so: he keeps his purposes to himself for ages, and watches with indifference as wickedness triumphs over good. Is it only after such a long time that God has remembered to judge the life of men? Did he not care before?[70] They babble about God day and night in their impious and sullied way; they arouse the awe of the illiterate with their false descriptions of the punishments awaiting those who have sinned. Thus they behave like the guardians of the Bacchic mysteries, who never tire of talking about the phantoms and terrors that await those who reveal the secrets to outsiders.[71]

They postulate, for example, that their messiah will return as a conqueror on the clouds, and that he will rain fire upon the earth in his battle with the princes of the air, and that the whole world, with the exception of believing Christians, will be consumed in fire.[72] An interesting idea—and hardly an original one. The idea came from the Greeks and others—namely, that after cycles of years and because of the fortuitous conjunctions of certain stars there are conflagrations and floods, and that after the last flood, in the time of Deucalion, the cycle demands a conflagration in accordance with the alternating succession of the universe. This is responsible for the silly opinion of some Christians that God will come down and rain fire upon the earth.

But what kind of God is it who "comes down" to earth and brings fire along with him? As Plato has taught,[73] God is that which is beautiful and happy and exists within himself in the most perfect of all conceivable states. This means that God is changeless. A god who comes down to men undergoes change—a change from good to bad; from beautiful to shameful; from happiness to misfortune; from what is perfect to what is wicked. Now what sort of a god

would choose a change like that? Is it not rather the essence of a mortal to undergo change and remolding, and
the nature of an immortal being to remain the same without alteration? Accordingly, it cannot be the case that God
came down to earth, since in so doing he would have
undergone an alteration of his nature.

To be blunt: Either God really does change as they suggest into a human being (and this, as noted, is an impossibility), or else he does not change, but rather makes them
who see him think that he is only mortal, and so deceives
them, and tells lies—which it is not the nature of a god to
do.[74] Deceit and lying are in all other cases wrong, except
only when one uses them as a sort of medicine for friends
who are sick and mad, in order to heal them—or in the case
of enemies when one is trying to escape danger. But then,
no sick or mad man is God's friend, nor is God afraid of
anyone to the extent that he should have to resort to trickery to avoid them.

The Jews say that as life is filled with all manner of evil,
it is necessary for God to send someone down so that the
wicked may be punished and everything purified, as it
was when the first flood occurred. The Christians add
other ideas to these, but the central point is the same:
namely, that God is vindictive and repentant. Who can
doubt that the God who destroyed the tower of Babel
desired to purify the earth of disobedience, just as did the
God who sent the flood? And like Phaeton of old, so does
he undertake to destroy Sodom and Gommorah by fire on
account of their sins. Such a god seems to delight in re-
penting of what he has created and—having lost control
over it—in reducing it to rubble.[75] The Christians have
added to the ancient myths of destruction the idea that the
Son of God has already come down to earth—because of
the sins of the Jews—and that because the Jews punished
Jesus and gave him gall and vinegar to drink, they brought
down on their heads the full fury of God's wrath.

As to the squabbles of the Jews and the Christians, I can only say that these sects remind me of a cluster of bats or ants escaping from a nest, a bunch of frogs holding council in a swamp, or a clutch of worms assembling in the muck: all of them disagreeing over who is the worst sinner. Thus do they say "God shows himself to us first—and he ignores the affairs of the world in order to give us, his chosen, his full attention; he sends his messengers to us alone, and never stops sending them and seeking that we may dwell with him forever." And the wormlike Christians say, "Well, you are wrong, because in the rankings God is first and we fall next since we are made exactly in God's image and all things have been put under us— earth, water, air, stars, and the rest—everything exists for our benefit and to serve only us. Since some remain outside the fold, God will send his son to consume the unrighteous so that we—the saved—can have eternal life with him."[76] So much for the message of the Jews and Christians. Would not such assertions be more forgivable coming from worms and frogs than from these sects in their petty squabbles?

And who are the Jews? They are runaway slaves who escaped from Egypt. They never did anything of importance—they have never been of any significance or prominence whatever, for nothing of their history is to be found in the Greek histories. They have tried in their holy books—shamefully I may add—to trace their genealogy back to the first offspring of sorcerers and deceivers, invoking the witness of vague and ambiguous utterances concealed in dark obscurity. And this they have put across to the uneducated and to the gullible in spite of the fact that throughout the span of history no such idea has been expressed. In days gone by other peoples have made such claims: the Athenians, the Egyptians, the Arcadians, and the Phrygians—who maintain that some of their ancestors were born of the earth, and try to prove such assertions.[77]

Of course, being cornered in the insignificant land of Palestine, we cannot expect the Jews to have heard the stories and fables sung in poetry by Hesiod and other inspired men. And so they contrived for themselves a crude and fantastic story about man being formed by God and breathed on by God, and that a woman was then formed out of the man's right side, and that God gave them commands, and that a serpent came and proved himself superior to the wishes of God.[78] This legend they tell the old women—as if to publicize the fact that their God is a weakling from the start—indeed, wholly unable to control even the first-made of his creatures.

Now it is true that the more reasonable among the Jews and Christians are ashamed of this nonsense and try their best to allegorize it, as with the stories related by Hesiod. How else are we to understand the story about creating woman from the man's rib[79]—which indeed in its literal form is only fit for the ears of old women. So too their fantastic story—which they take from the Jews—concerning the flood and the building of an enormous ark,[80] and the business about the message brought back to the survivors of the flood by a dove (or was it an old crow?). This is nothing more than a debased and nonsensical version of the myth of Deucalion, a fact I am sure they would not want to come to light. As it stands, the story is really one for the hearing of small children.

To move to other fables: There is also current among the Christians a variety of stories dealing with the begetting of children long after the parents are of child-bearing age.[81] Their books are chock full of stories about the treacheries of mothers, God appearing on earth in various disguises, brother murdering brother, purportedly righteous men having intercourse with various women other than their wives; indeed, stories that rival in their immorality the tales of the Thyestians: brothers selling brothers, women being turned into salt—and so on. It is no wonder that the reasonable among the Christians, embarrassed as they ought to be by such stories, take refuge in allegory!—as they are, all in all, very stupid fables. On the other hand, some of the allegories I have seen are even more ridiculous than the myths themselves, since they attempt to explain the fables by means of ideas that really do not fit into the context of the stories. I myself know a story of this sort entitled "The Controversy between Papiscus and Jason", an allegory so absurd that it does not merit my ridicule but rather my pity and contempt.[82] I think it is unnecessary to refute this sort of stuff, as its silliness will be apparent to anyone who has the patience to read through it. Instead of ridiculing Christian tracts, I would much prefer to say something positive about the natural world and its order—to teach, for example, that there is no god worthy of the name who created mortals: whatever god there is, he must have made immortal beings, and mortal beings are their handiwork, as the Philosopher teaches.[83]

As the soul is the work of a god, so the body is by nature different—not to be distinguished from the body of a bat, a worm, or a frog. We are all—all of us—made of the same matter; and we are all—all of us—destined for corruption, despite what the Christians teach us to the contrary. Again, it must be said that with respect to the body all animals have a single common nature; this nature passes through changes and subsists in many different forms, returning in the end to what it originally was; yet no product of matter is immortal.[84]

I turn now to consider the existence of evil,[85] which is analogous to matter itself in that there can be no decrease or increase of evils in the world—neither in the past nor in the future. From the beginning of time, the beginning of the universe, there has been just so much evil, and in quantity it has remained the same.[86] It is in the nature of the universe that this be the case, and depends on our understanding the origins of the universe itself. Certainly

someone who has no learning in philosophy will be unaware of the origin of evil; but it is enough that the masses
be told that evils are not caused by God;[87] rather, that they
are a part of the nature of matter and of mankind; that the
period of mortal life is the same from beginning to end,
and that because things happen in cycles, what is happen-
ing now—evils that is—happened before and will happen
again.[88] Yet while evil persists, the whole picture is rather
different from what we see of the visible world: each thing
comes into being and dies for the good of the whole—
according to the processes of change of which I previously
wrote. What this means theologically is that neither good
nor evil can possibly increase on earth: God has no need of
[what the Christians call] a new creation;[89] God does not
inflict correction on the world as if he were an unskilled
laborer who is incapable of building something properly
first time around; God has no need to purify what he has
built by means of a flood or a conflagration (as they teach).

There is a sort of arrogance in the assumption of the
Christians that evil is on the rise. Even if something seems
evil to you it is far from clear whether it is really evil; one
person with his limited perspective on the whole state of
creation is unequipped to know whether what is good for
you is good for someone else in the universe, and vice
versa. When a man was angry with the Jews and killed
them all, both young and old, and burned down their city,
they were completely annihilated; yet (they say) when the
supreme God was angry and wrathful he sent his son with
threats—and suffered all kinds of indignities.[90]

I shall have to show that their stupidity really hinges on
their doctrine of creation, since they hold that God made
all things for the sake of men, whereas our philosophy
maintains that the world was made as much for the benefit
of the irrational animals as for men[91]—I mean, why *should*
things have been created more for man's nourishment
than for the benefit of the plants and trees, the grass and

the thorns? I suppose they ignore the fact that things do not grow without human endeavor—we struggle to make things fertile, whatever God may have to do with the case—whereas they attribute everything to God as though everything grew without sowing and tillage. As Euripides says, "Sun and light serve mortals"[92] but they serve the ants and flies as well. For in their case, too, the night is for sleeping and the day for doing.

The Christians, like the Jews, boast that we are the rulers and Lords of creation—because we hunt and feast on animals. I might reply by asking why rather they are not our masters, and why it cannot be said that we were made for their sake, since they also hunt and feed on us. And while they go to hunt alone, we tend to need dogs, weapons, and other men to help us against the prey! And so to those who say that man is superior to the irrational animals, I reply that God indeed gave us the ability to catch the wild beasts and to make use of them; yet it is also true that before there were cities, arts, culture, weapons, and nets—men were captured and eaten by the wild beasts, and it was rarely the other way round. And if it is said that human beings are better than the irrational animals because we live in cities and occupy prominent offices and the like—I say this proves nothing: ants and bees do as much; or at any rate, the bees elect leaders and a stratified social system of leaders, attendants, servants; they have their weapons and wage their wars, slay the vanquished, build cities and even suburbs. They share in the work of their society and punish the idlers—that is to say, in driving out the drones to fend for themselves. And the ants are no less clever, for they pick out the unripened fruit for themselves to keep it through the year—and set a place apart as a graveyard for those of their number who have died.[93] Indeed, the very ants meet in council to plan strategy; this is why they do not lose their way. They have a fully developed intelligence—and it seems they have as well a clear-cut notion of certain universal laws, and even a voice to make the experience of their learning known to others of their kind.

In view of all this, I ask the Christians: If someone were to look out from heaven down upon the earth, what difference would he see between what we do and what the ants and bees do? Perhaps it will be said that human beings have learned magical arts and sorcery, and that this the animals can never have. I reply that in this regard the snakes and bees have done us one better, for it is clear that they know the antidotes to diseases and preventions for many more—including the use of stone to keep their young from harm. Let a man get hold of such secrets and he will think he has something marvelous—yet the animals know the secrets already.

Next let it be said by some unthinking Christian that it is our ability to conceive of a deity—to think about God—that sets us apart from the "lower" creatures. But I ask whether it is so—the power of divination is a case in point, and this man must learn from the birds and other animals. It would seem that there are animals of special use to prophets—call them "prophetic animals" if you will—but in any case the power of foreknowledge has been given them by God, and they in turn impart this knowledge to men. This being so, it is clear that these animals are much nearer to God—perhaps they are wiser than we and dearer to God than we. Some say that the birds have associations similar to our own secret societies and that they can read what the birds say and that having gotten information about such and such an event from the birds, things turned out just as the birds had predicted. It is said further that no animal is able to keep an oath better than an elephant, and for that reason the elephant is more faithful to God than many men are. So too, the stork is more pious than many a man, and more affectionate, as the young storks bring food to their parents. An Arabian bird, the phoenix, spends many a day seeking out the body of its father in Egypt, and will bury its father in a ball of myrrh in the shrine of the sun.[94]

From all this it can be seen that all things have not been made for man—any more than for the lion, the eagle, or the dolphin—but rather all has been made by God so that the world itself may be complete and perfect in all its parts. Things have indeed been proportioned, but not for the sake of man—rather for the good of the universe as a whole. God takes care of the universe; that is to say, providence never abandons it, and it does not become more evil. The Christians are silly to say, therefore, that God turns the world back to himself after a period of neglect,[95] nor does he become angry because man "sins"—any more than he is angry with monkeys and mice for doing what they do naturally. For each has his allotted place in the scheme of things.

VI. ON JEWS AND CHRISTIANS

I now turn to exhort the Jews and Christians, but most especially the Christians: No god or son of God has come down to earth; nor would anyone deserving of the name God have come down to earth. Or do you mean not a god but some angel or demon? Or do you mean (as I assume you do) some other sort of being?

One thing about the Jews is worth noting: although they worship the heavens and the angels in it, yet they reject paying homage to its most sacred parts, namely the sun, moon, and the other stars—both fixed and mobile. They behave as though the whole could be God and yet in its individual parts not be divine. Or else they seem to think that one ought to worship beings that descend among people who are blinded by darkness, perhaps as a result of magical arts of some kind, or people who have nightmares. But as for those beings who foretell the future so clearly—I mean the beings that tell the coming of the showers, the heat, the clouds (which they worship), the lightnings, and all the productivity of nature—the very beings in short by whom God is revealed to them, and the clearest proof of the divinity above us—these they pay no heed to at all and hold for worthless.

It is equally silly of these Christians to suppose that when their God applies the fire (like a common cook!) all the rest of mankind will be thoroughly roasted, and that they alone will escape unscorched—not just those alive at the time, mind you, but (they say) those long since dead will rise up from the earth possessing the same bodies as they did before.[96] I ask you: Is this not the hope of worms? For what sort of human soul is it that has any use for a rotted corpse of a body? The very fact that some Jews and even some Christians[97] reject this teaching about rising corpses shows just how utterly repulsive it is: it is nothing less than nauseating and impossible. I mean, what sort of body is it that could return to its original nature or become the same as it was before it rotted away? And of course they have no reply for this one, and as in most cases where there *is* no reply they take cover by saying "Nothing is impossible with God."[98] A brilliant answer indeed! But the fact is, God cannot do what is shameful; and God does not do what is contrary to nature. If, in your evildoing, you were to ask God to do something terrible, God could not do it—and hence you ought not believe, as so many of them do, that every base desire is to be fulfilled for the asking. For God is not the answer to every whimsical request; he does not deal in confusion. He is the creator of what is by nature just and true and right. He may, as Heracleitus says, be able to provide everlasting life for a soul; but the same philosopher notes that "corpses should be disposed of like dung, for dung they are."[99] As for the body—so full of corruption and other sorts of nastiness—God could not (and would not) make it everlasting, as this is contrary to reason. For he himself is the Logos—the reason—behind everything that exists, and he is not able to do anything that violates or contradicts his own character.[100]

Now, as to the Jews: they became an individual nation and made laws according to the custom of their people. They still maintain these laws among themselves to the present day and observe certain rites and practices which, though peculiar, have a grounding in ancient tradition. They are, in this regard anyway, no different from the rest of mankind: each nation follows its customs and laws, whatever they happen to be. This situation seems to have come to pass not only because certain people decided to think in a certain way and then went about devising ways to protect their social conventions, but also because from the beginning of the world different parts of the earth were allotted to different guardians, and, its having been apportioned in this manner, things are done in such a way as pleases the guardians. For this reason it is impious to abandon the customs which have existed in each locality from the beginning.

But the Christians are not like the Jews in this regard: I ask them where they came from, or who is the author of their traditional laws. "Nobody," they say, though it is the case that they originated from the Jews. Nor can they name any other source for their teacher and chorus-leader. Yet are they Jews? No—they rebelled against the Jews.

Herodotus writes as follows: "The people of the cities of Marea and Apis who live in the part of Egypt bordering on Libya, and thinking of themselves as Libyans instead of Egyptians, objected to the worship of the temples, not wishing to abstain from eating cows. So they sent to Ammon, saying that they had nothing in common with the Egyptians, as they lived outside the delta and did not agree with them. They wanted Ammon to allow them to taste all meats, but the god did not allow them to do this,

saying that the land which the Nile passed over was
Egypt, and that those who lived below the city of Elephan-
tine and drank from this river were Egyptians."[101] Thus
says Herodotus. Now I submit that Herodotus is no less
equipped to give an account of the things of God than the
angels of the Jews; thus there is nothing wrong if each
nation observes its own laws of worship, and actually we
find that the difference between the nations is quite considerable, though (naturally) each thinks its way of doing
things is by far the best. To wit: the Egyptians who live at
Meroe worship only Zeus and Dionysus. The Arabians
worship only Ourania and Dionysus. The Egyptians all
worship Osiris and Isis; the people of Sais, Athena; the
Naucratites—of recent vintage—worship Serapis, and so
with the rest of us according to our respective laws:[102]
Some abstain from sheep, reverencing them as sacred;
others stay away from goats, others from crocodiles, still
others from cows or from pigs, for they abhor being con-
taminated by them. Among the Scythian peoples cannibalism prospers, and some Indians consider it an act of
piety to eat their fathers. To continue with what Herodotus says (quoting verbatim from him in the interest of
accuracy), he tells the following story:[103] "If someone
were to call a council of all men and tell them to choose
what laws are best, doubtless each after some thought—
not much—would choose his own. Therefore it is not likely that anyone but a lunatic would make a mockery of
these things: all men always have believed their way."
There are yet other witnesses to how much men have
believed their laws were the only laws: while he ruled,
Darius called the Greeks who were with him and asked
how much money it would take for them to eat their dead
fathers; they answered that they would not do such a
thing at any price. He then called those called Calatians
(Indians) who do feed on their fathers, and asked them (in
the presence of the Greeks and through an interpreter)
how much he would have to pay them to cremate their

dead fathers rather than eat them. But they shouted aloud in a fury at the very suggestion, until he commanded them to keep silence. Such is the power of custom and law; as Pindar says, "Custom is the king of all."[104] Accordingly there is nothing wrong with a very ancient people like the Jews maintaining their laws; the fault is rather with those who have abandoned their own traditions in order to profess those of the Jews—those who act as though they have had some deeper revelation that entitles them to turn away from their friends and countrymen on the pretext that they have reached a higher level of piety and have heard that their doctrine of heaven is not original with them but (just for an example) was held long ago by the Persians. Their habit, writes Herodotus, is to go up to the highest peaks of the mountains to offer sacrifice to Zeus and indeed to call the whole circle of heaven Zeus.[105] I think, therefore, that it is of little importance whether we call Zeus "The Most High" or Zen or Adonai or Sabaoth or Amoun (like the Egyptians) or Papaeus, like the Scythians. Moreover, they would certainly not be holier than other people just because they are circumcised, since others, such as the Egyptians and the Colchians, did this before them. They are not holier just because they abstain from pigs—the Egyptians did this before them as well, as also from goats, sheep, oxen, and fish. And the Pythagoreans abstain from beans and all living things. Nor is it really likely that the Jews are God's chosen people and are loved more than other folk, or that the angels are sent only to them—as though they had been given some land set aside just for themselves. We can see what sort of land it is that God thought worthy of them! And we see what sort of people inhabit it! Well, enough about the Jews; I shall leave off, remarking only that they do not know the great God, but they have been deceived by Moses' sorcery and have learned that without availing themselves anything at all.[106]

Let us turn instead to the renegades from Judaism, the

Christians, those led on by the sorcery of Moses and seduced by their god, Jesus. I do not wish to discuss the silly
and contradictory things they have to say about their
teacher. I am willing even to assume that he really was an
angel. But in that case, can we say he is the first of his kind
ever to have come? Were there not others before him? If
they say he is unique, then they are telling lies and contra-
dicting themselves. For they admit that others have come,
fifty or sixty at once, and were punished by being cast
under the earth in chains, which they say are full of hot
springs made hot by the tears of the tormented.[107] They
say as well that an angel came to the tomb of this man—
some say one, some two—who replied to the women that
he was risen.[108] It seems that the Son of God was not able
to move the stone, but needed an angel to do it for him.[109]
Not only that, but an angel came to the carpenter to defend Mary when she was pregnant, and another angel
appeared to tell them that they must run for their lives to
save the infant from danger.[110] It seems useless for me to
provide a complete list of all those said to have appeared
to Moses and others. The point is, of course, that this
Jesus is hardly the only angelic being reckoned to have
visited mankind; even before his time there are those who
were sent by the creator, though some among the Christians—Marcion and his disciple Apelles for example—
think that the creator is an inferior god.[111] On this point
there is considerable disagreement, for while some of the
Christians proclaim they have the same god as do the
Jews, others insist that there is another god higher than
the creator-god and opposed to him. And some Christians
teach that the Son came from this higher god. Still others
admit of a third god—those, that is to say, who call themselves gnostics[112]—and still others, though calling themselves Christians, want to live according to the laws of the
Jews.[113] I could also mention those who call themselves
Simonians after Simon,[114] and those naming themselves

Helenians after Helen,[115] his consort. There are Christian sects named after Marcellina,[116] Harpocratian Christians who trace themselves to Salome,[117] some who follow Mariamne and others who follow Martha,[118] and still others who call themselves Marcionites after their leader, Marcion. Pretty clearly, some put their faith in one god, others in another; but all in all they walk around in a fog, so evil and murky that it rivals the feasts of Antinous in Egypt. Thus is the extent of their evil and their ignorance. Christians, it is needless to say, utterly detest each other;[119] they slander each other constantly with the vilest forms of abuse, and cannot come to any sort of agreement in their teaching. Each sect brands its own, fills the head of its own with deceitful nonsense, and makes perfect little pigs of those it wins over to its side. Like so many sirens they chatter away endlessly and beat their breasts: The world (they say to their shame) is crucified to me, and I to the world.

There are some few who claim to know more than the Jews. Let it be so: let us assume that even though they have no authority for their doctrine their teaching bears examining—and let us examine it. Let's speak about their systematic corruption of the truth, their misunderstanding of some fairly simple philosophical principles—which of course they completely botch.

VII. CRITIQUE OF CHRISTIAN DOCTRINE

Many of the ideas of the Christians have been expressed better—and earlier—by the Greeks, who were however modest enough to refrain from saying that their ideas came from a god or a son of God. The ancients in their wisdom revealed certain truths to those able to understand: Plato, son of Ariston, points to the truth about the highest good when he says that it cannot be expressed in words, but rather comes from familiarity—like a flash from the blue, imprinting itself upon the soul.[120] But even if Plato were wrong—even if the highest good could be expressed in writing or in words, then would it not be equally good—indeed what could be better—to reveal this for the benefit of all men? As for Plato, he held that the good is known to a few; for when the masses get a hold of some sacred truth, or half truth, they behave arrogantly and contemptuously towards one another.[121] But Plato, having said this, doesn't go on to record some myth to make his point (as do so many others), nor does he silence the inquirer who questions some of the truths he professes; Plato does not ask people to stop questioning, or to accept that God is like such-and-such or has a son named so-and-so, to whom I was just talking this morning! I shall belabor my point a bit, but in doing so I hope to make myself clearer.

Anyone knows that there is such a thing as true doctrine. This should be obvious to anyone who undertakes to write about such things. Everything that is, all that exists, has three things that make knowledge of it possible. The knowledge of the thing itself is generally regarded as a fourth attribute. The fifth attribute is that which is knowable and true. To put it in Plato's language: the first is the name; the second, the word; the third, the image; the fourth, knowledge.[122] In so defining the good, Plato does indeed stress that it cannot be described in words; but he gives ample reason for this difficulty in order to avoid putting discussion of the good beyond question and discussion. Even the nature of Nothing could be described in words.

Now Plato is not speaking in vain; he does not dissimulate or claim that he is saying something new. Plato does not claim that he descended from heaven to announce his doctrines. Rather, he tells us where his doctrines come from; there is, in short, a history to what he says, and he is happy to point to the sources of his knowledge, instead of asking us to believe that he speaks on his own authority.

What do the Christians say? They say, "First believe that the person who tells us these things is God's son, even though he was arrested and humiliated, punished in the sight of all, and wandered about preaching in mean circumstances. This is all the more reason to believe!"[123] So say the Christians. Now if these believers confess Jesus and others confess someone else, and if they all together have the slogan "Believe and be saved, or damn you," what is to happen to those who really do want to be saved? I mean, which path are they to follow, since advice of the same sort is coming from all quarters? Are the ones who crave salvation to throw dice in order to find out where they should turn? How much should they gamble on their salvation? Whom should they follow? The Christians appeal to the worst of these salvation-hungry people by insisting that the wisdom of men is nothing but foolishness with God,[124] and thus do they attempt to bring into their fold the uneducated and stupid. (I might mention that even on this point they are merely plagiarizing the ideas of the Greek philosophers, who long ago taught that human wisdom is one thing, divine wisdom another.) And did not Heracleitus teach that "The character of man has no common sense, but that of God has." And, further, "A man is no more than a fool before God, as a child is before a man."[125] And the great Plato, in his *Apology*, said: "I, men of Athens, have come to have the name I have because of wisdom; and what sort of wisdom is it? It is that wisdom which a man may have, and in this way I am, I should say, wise."[126] It can be seen that even the Christian distinction between God's wisdom and man's goes back to Heracleitus and Plato. But the Christians mean something more by making this distinction. They pitch their message to the uneducated, the slaves, and the ignorant—those wholly without wisdom—and then convince them that the wisdom they possess in their newfound superstition is divine—the wisdom of God himself! This may be seen in the fact that they run away at a gallop from people of learning and culture—people whom they cannot deceive—and trap illiterate people instead.[127]

Not surprisingly, they emphasize the virtue of humility (which in their case is to make a virtue of necessity!) here again prostituting the noble ideas of Plato, who writes in the Laws: "God, who knows the beginning and middle and end of all that is, advances in a straight course according to nature; justice follows the transgressor, and he who is happy follows the divine law closely and humbly."[128] Now it is one thing to follow the divine law with humility, knowing the wisdom with which it has been ordained. Christian humility is something else again: for in Christianity the "humble" man demeans himself in a humiliating fashion, throwing himself headlong upon the ground; crawling on his knees; garbing himself like a beggar in rags; smearing himself with the dirt of the road.

Not only do they misunderstand the words of the philosophers; they even stoop to assigning words of the philosophers to their Jesus. For example, we are told that Jesus judged the rich with the saying "It is easier for a camel to go through the eye of a needle than for a rich man to enter the Kingdom of God."[129] Yet we know that Plato expressed this very idea in a purer form when he said, "It is impossible for an exceptionally good man to be exceptionally rich."[130] Is one utterance more inspired than the other?

And what of their belief in a trinity of gods; is not even this central doctrine of theirs a gross misinterpretation of certain things Plato says in his letters? "All things," writes the philosopher, "are centered on the King of the All; and the All is for his sake, and he is the cause of all that is good. The secondary things are centered in the Second, and the third things are centered in the Third."[131] The human soul wants to learn about these things and to discover their true nature, by looking at things related to itself—none of which are perfect. But with respect to the king and the principles, there is nothing imperfect. It is because these Christians have completely misunderstood the words of Plato that they boast of God as above the heavens and put him higher than the heavens in which the Jews believe. But no earthly poet, and truly no Christian, has described or sung the regions of heaven as befits them: ultimate being, Plato calls it; "colorless, formless, untouchable, and visible only to the mind that guides the soul in its quest for the true knowledge that inhabits this sphere."[132]

Now the Christians pray that after their toil and strife here below they shall enter the kingdom of heaven, and they agree with the ancient systems that there are seven heavens and that the way of the soul is through the planets. That their system is based on very old teachings may be seen from similar beliefs in the old Persian mysteries associated with the cult of Mithras. In that system there is an orbit for the fixed stars, another for the planets and a diagram for the passage of the soul through the latter. They picture this as a ladder with seven gates, and at the very top an eighth gate: the first gate is lead, the second tin, the third bronze, the fourth iron, the fifth an alloy, the sixth silver, and the seventh gold. And they associate the metals with the gods as follows: the lead with Kronos, taking lead to symbolize his slowness; the second with Aphrodite, comparing the tin with her brightness and softness; the third with Zeus—the bronze symbolizing the firmness of the god; the fourth with Hermes, for both iron and Hermes are reliable and hard-working; the fifth with Ares—the gate which as a result of mixture is uneven in quality; the sixth with the moon; and the seventh with the sun—the last two being symbolized by the colors of the metals.[133]

Of course, were one to lay the cosmology of the Persians alongside that of the Christians, one could see the differences between them, since I have seen a Christian drawing in which there were ten circles, separated from one another and held together by a single circle said to be the soul of the universe, called Leviathan.[134] The diagram was divided by a thick black line which, I was told, was Gehenna or Tartarus.[135]

These Christians also speak of a seal, given by the father to a young man called the Son or the Son of Man, who claims to have been anointed with a white ointment from the tree of life.[136] The Christians teach that when a man is dying, seven angels stand alongside the soul, one group being angels of light, the remainder being what are called archontic angels, and the head of these archons is said to be the angel accursed of God. Some Christians [that is, the Gnostics] maintain that it is the god of the Jews who is the accursed angel, and that it is this god who sends thunder, who created the world and was worshipped by Moses, who describes his actions in his own story of the creation of the world.[137] Well, such a god may well deserve to be accursed if he is the god who cursed the serpent for granting man the knowledge of good and evil![138]

What could be sillier than what the Christians call wisdom![139] The god of the Jews, their great lawgiver (say the Christians) made a mistake.[140] Be it so: then why do you accept his laws as being worth following—why take these laws and interpret them as allegories? Why do you so grudgingly worship this Creator, you hypocrites, when he promised the Jews everything—that he would make their race prosper, that he would raise them up from the dead in their own flesh and blood—this same God who inspired the prophets? Yet you pour abuse on him! But when you Christians find things made difficult for you by the Jews, you come around and say that you worship the same God as they do! What is to be believed? For when your master, Jesus, lays down laws contrary to those laid down by Moses, in whom the Jews put their faith, you immediately undertake to find another God, one who is different from the Father.[141]

Some of the Christians, like the followers of other mysteries, carry their theories to the point of absurdity, heaping the sayings of oracles on top of other sayings, all designed to confuse. And so we hear of circles on top of circles and emanations flowing out of emanations, earthly churches and churches of the circumcision; we witness the Jews flowing from a power represented as a virgin—Prunicus (Sophia)[142]—and another living soul who was killed so that heaven could have life. Or they show the earth slain with a sword, or men slain so that others may live, and they show the evil of death being put to an end when the sin of the world is slain. They also depict in their diagrams a narrow passageway through the spheres, and gates that open of their own accord. These same Christians never tire of speaking of the "Tree of Life" and of resurrection of the flesh made possible by the tree—the symbolism being obvious if we accept their story that their master was nailed to a tree and was a carpenter by trade. I suspect that had he been thrown off a cliff or pushed into a pit or strangled—or had he been instead of a carpenter a cobbler, stonemason, or blacksmith, we would find them telling tales of a cliff of life in the heavens, or a pit of the resurrection, or a rope of immortality, or a blessed stone, or the smelter of love, or the holy hide of leather. I wonder, would not even a drunken old crone who sang such stories to a baby as lullabies be embarrassed by them?

But that is not the most remarkable thing about these Christians: They interpret certain words that appear inscribed between the upper circles, above the heavens, a larger and a smaller in particular, as the Son and the Father, and they teach their converts to read the signs and learn the interpretation of the diagrams, promising that in so doing they will become proficient in sorcery. They are really very dishonest, borrowing even their incantations from other religions in their magic acts. Their real talent is in hoodwinking people who are ignorant of the fact that the demons have different names among the Greeks, the Scythians, and so on (as Herodotus teaches us when he recounts that the Scythians call Apollo Gongosyrus, Poseidon, Thagimasada; Aphrodite, Agrimpasa; and Hestia, Tabitha.[143] I shall not here go into their crazy displays of pretended power: it is enough to comment on the fact that countless persons have sought comfort for their sins by recourse to such religious chicanery; countless religions have promised to purge men's souls; countless charlatans have promised to deliver the gullible from evil and disease; and yes, these Christian healers and magic-doers are able to produce noisy crashes and effects; they pretend to do miracles in Jesus' name;[144] they conjure by means of silks and curtains, numbers, stones, plants and the assorted paraphernalia that one expects of such people—roots and objects of all sorts.

Though they profess faith, I have seen these Christian priests use books containing magical formulas and the names of various demons; they surely are up to no good, but only mean to deceive good people by these tricks of theirs. I have this first hand, from an Egyptian musician by the name of Dionysus. He testifies that magical ploys are especially effective among the illiterate and among those with shady moral characters.[145] Those who have had anything to do with philosophy, on the other hand, are above such trickery, since they are interested in examining actions and looking at their consequences.

Their utter stupidity can be illustrated in any number of ways, but especially with reference to their misreading of the divine enigmas and their insistence that there exists a being opposed to God, whom they know by the name of devil (in Hebrew, Satanas, for they refer to one and the same being by various names). But they show how utterly concocted these ideas are when they go on to say that the highest god in heaven, desiring to do such and such—say, confer some great gift on man—cannot fulfill his purpose because he is opposed and thwarted by a god who is his opposite. Does this mean that the Son of God can be beaten by a devil? Do they really mean that the Son of God is punished by the devil as some kind of lesson, as if to teach us that we should be indifferent to the punishments to be inflicted upon us? They teach even that Satan will manifest himself again and will show his works to mankind, rivaling God in his power and glory.[146] To this they say that we should not be led astray by the works of the devil, but rather should stick close to the Christian God and believe in him alone. What blasphemy is this? Is it not patently the sort of thing one would expect to hear from a magician, a sorcerer who is out only for his own gain, and teaching that his rival magicians are working their wonders by the power of evil, while he and he alone represents the power of good? What else could we expect of these beggars?[147]

Now, what is the source of their opinions? If we look to Heracleitus, we find the following: "War is a mutual thing, and justice is no more than strife: everything that exists has come to be through strife and necessity."[148] Pherecydes, even earlier than Heracleitus, tells of two armies set to do battle, Kronos heading one side, Ophioneus leading the opposing side. They agree after much deliberation that whichever army is driven into the ocean (*Ogenus*) should be the vanquished, while that which succeeds in driving the other into the pit should inherit the heavens.[149] We find a similar myth promulgated in the stories of the Titans and the Giants and in the mysteries related by the Egyptians concerning Typhon, Horus and Osiris.[150] Confronted with such stories, we are first to inquire of their meaning, and it is clear that the ancients were not telling tales about devils and demons. Homer writes as follows of the words spoken by Hephaestus to Hera: "Once when I was ready to defend you, he took me by the foot and threw me down from the heavenly places."[151] Zeus speaks to Hera as follows, "Do you remember when you were hanging on high, and I attached anvils to his legs and cast unbroken chains of gold about your arms? You were hanging in the ether of clouds. Then the gods struck—far from Olympus—but even though standing next to him, they could not free him. No, but I, seizing him, pitched him from the threshold of heaven, and he fell helplessly to earth."[152] Now the words of Zeus to Hera are not to be taken at face value. They refer to God's words to matter; they point vaguely to the fact that at the beginning everything was in chaos and that God divided the world into certain sectors, put it together, and organized the whole. He cast away all the arrogant archons (putting them on earth). Thus does Pherecydes understand Homer when he says, "Beneath that land is the land of Tartarus, guarded by the daughters of Boreas, the Harpies and Thyella; and Zeus casts away any god if he becomes arrogant."[153] This is the meaning of the procession of the Panathenaea, when Athena's robe is paraded; it signifies that an unmothered and undefiled goddess rules the arrogant rulers of the earth. So should myths be read.

But the Christian notion that the Son of God accepted the punishments inflicted upon him by a devil is merely ludicrous, especially if we are to think that this is to teach us to endure punishments quietly.[154] In my view the Son of God had a right to punish the devil; he certainly had no reason to threaten with punishment the men he came to save,[155] the very ones who had suffered so much from the devil's abuse. It is even clear where they get their idea of a son of God. For in the old days men used to call this world of ours the child of God and personify it as a demigod, in as much as it originated from God. Jesus and the "child" of God are very much alike. But the ancients were speaking figuratively; the Christians think of Jesus as the very Logos of God. And their world-view is very silly—as silly, in fact, as their record of how man came to be:

They teach that man existed first in a garden planted by God, and that after a time man was thrown out of this garden, due to certain circumstances beyond his control, and was made to live in a world that in most respects was the very opposite of the garden. Now all of this is very silly indeed. Moses can only have written such things because he was stupid, and their general effect is like that of the old comedies, where we hear: "Proteus married Bellerophon, and Pegasus came from Arcadia."[156] In short, Moses and the prophets who put together this record had absolutely no inkling how the world came to be, and their books are absolute garbage. All that business about "Let there be light"—Are we to think that the creator of the world used light from above like a man who borrows a torch from his neighbor? Or are we to think, as do some Christians, that a demonic god made the world contrary to the will of the good god; and if so, why was the light not snuffed out from the start? I shall not here enter into questions of physics—whether the world is uncreated and indestructible or created and destructible. But we do not teach that the creator is a stranger to the world. Some among the Christians say that things were devised by a creator different from the great God who rules supreme, and that the great God restrained himself from acting, but can no longer do so;[157] and they go on to teach that creation needs to be destroyed. Some teach that when the great God has given the spirit to the Creator he asks for it to be returned. But what sort of god is this? What god asks for something he has given to be returned to him—for to ask for something is the action of one who is in need, and God, by definition, needs nothing. If the great God lent his spirit, was he unaware that he was lending it to an evil being? And if the good god and the creator are opposing principles, why does the good god endure with an evil god who opposes him? These Christians I would query as follows: Why does (the good god) wish to destroy the creations of the creator? Why does he impose himself as he does, by cunning and deceit? Why does he steal away those people whom the creator has cursed, and deal with mankind like a slave dealer? If they are the creator's work, why does he teach them to escape from their master? If the creator is their father, why must they flee from home? And what right, lacking consent of the parent, does he have to steal them away from their father?[158] Well, what have we in the end? An impressive god indeed: one who desires nothing more than to adopt sinners as his children; one who takes to himself the creatures who stand condemned by another, the poor wretches who are (as they say of themselves) naught but dung; a god who is not capable of taking vengeance on this creator, but falls prey to him after sending out his son to do the dirty work.

But if these are truly the Creator's works, how can it be that God should make what is evil? How can he repent when they become ungrateful and wicked?[159] How can he find fault with his own handiwork, or threaten to destroy his own offspring? Where is he to banish them, out of the world that he himself has made?

Look further at the creation story credited among them, where we have read that God banishes man from the garden made specifically to contain him.[160] Silly as that may be, sillier still is the way the world is supposed to have come about. They allot certain days to creation, before days existed.[161] For when heaven had not been made, or the earth fixed or the sun set in the heavens, how could days exist? Isn't it absurd to think that the greatest God pieced out his work like a bricklayer, saying "Today I shall do this, tomorrow that," and so on, so that he did this on the third, that on the fourth, and something else on the fifth and sixth days! We are thus not surprised to find that, like a common workman, this God wears himself down and so needs a holiday after six days.[162] Need I comment that a god who gets tired, works with his hands, and gives orders like a foreman is not acting very much like a god?

VIII. THE CHRISTIAN DOCTRINE OF GOD

The Christians say that God has hands, a mouth, and a voice; they are always proclaiming that "God said this" or "God spoke." "The heavens declare the work of his hands," they say.[163] I can only comment that such a God is no god at all, for God has neither hands, mouth, nor voice, nor any characteristics of which we know. And they say that God made man in his own image, failing to realize that God is not at all like a man, nor vice versa; God resembles no form known to us. They say that God has form, namely the form of the Logos, who became flesh in Jesus Christ.[164] But we know that God is without shape, without color. They say that God moved above the waters he created—but we know that it is contrary to the nature of God to move.[165] Their absurd doctrines even contain reference to God walking about in the garden he created for man; and they speak of him being angry, jealous, moved to repentance, sorry, sleepy—in short, as being in every respect more a man than a God. They have not read Plato, who teaches us in the *Republic* that God (the Good) does not even participate in being. It is true that all things are derived from the Good, as Plato says; but it is also clear that God made nothing mortal. This God of the philosophers is himself the underivable, the unnameable; he cannot be reached by reason. Such attributes as we may postulate of him are not the attributes of human nature, and all such attributes are quite distinct from his nature. He cannot be comprehended in terms of attributes or human

experience, contrary to what the Christians teach; moreover, he is outside any emotional experience.

It will be objected that this God taught by the philosophers cannot really be known: How can I know him? How
can one learn the way? Who will show him to me? It may
be objected that the philosopher's God is shrouded in
darkness, and that nothing can be known about him.
Here, too, we have instruction from Plato, who does indeed teach that, at first, we are in darkness concerning the
Good; but once led out of this darkness into the light, our
perception does not take well to the brilliance of its source;
rather, we think our sight is somehow damaged or inca-
pacitated.[166] But ask a Christian how God is known and
you will get a very different answer: for them the way is
not difficult, and they need not worry about the darkness
any longer. For them, the darkness has been expelled by
Jesus;[167] since God is hard to know, he cast his spirit into a
human body and journeyed down to earth so that we
might all be able to hear and learn from him.

The God of the philosophers need not resort to such
preposterous designs. Like the stoics, with whom we have
a great deal in common, we say that "God" is a spirit, and
like the Greeks we maintain that this spirit, so to speak,
permeates all things and contains all things within itself.[168] But the Christians say something very different:
they say that the Son of God possesses a spirit derived
from God, and that he was born in a human body; and
thus they teach that the Son of God is not himself immortal. Or would some Christians maintain that God himself
is not a spirit? Whatever they say, it is certain that there is
no such thing as a spirit that survives forever; it is not of
the nature of a spirit to do so. But the Christians hold the
simplistic view that God had poured out his spirit (in creation) and so needed to regain it. If this is so, then it is
impossible that Jesus rose bodily from the dead, for it
would have been impossible for God to have received back

his spirit once it had been defiled by coming into contact with human flesh. Moreover, if God wanted to send down a spirit from himself, why did he have to breathe into the womb of a woman?[169] I mean, he already knew how to make men without such contrivance. And presumably, he could have made an appropriate body for this occasion as well, without needing to befoul himself and his spirit. Had he been truly begotten from on high (as one of their gospels teaches) there might be more reason to believe their story.

And what proof do the Christians allege that this Jesus was the Son of God? Considering his punishment, how could he be proved divine, unless, of course, it was foretold that he should suffer and die as he did? But many Christians deny that his death was foretold.[170] These same Christians speak of two divine sons, locked in combat with one another. They fight like quails, the two sons, since their fathers are in their dotage and too tired to fight.

Now, as to the idea that the divine spirit was all locked up in a human body, we can assume that this body must certainly have differed from ours in size, beauty, strength, appeal, and the like. For it is plainly impossible that a body containing the essence of divinity itself would look just like anyone else's. But do they in fact say this? No. They claim that Jesus' body was just like the next man's, or was little, ugly, and repugnant.[171] Furthermore, if God (as in the portrayal of Zeus by the comic poet) woke up out of a long sleep and decided to deliver the human race from evils, one wonders why he sent this spirit of his only to some little backwater village of the Jews? Ought he not to have breathed into many bodies in the same way, the whole world over? The comic poet, to get a laugh, wrote that Zeus awoke and sent Hermes to the Athenians and Spartans. But I wonder, do you not find it a little ludicrous that the Christians take such a premise seriously: that the Son of God was sent only to the Jews.

IX. THE CHRISTIAN DOCTRINE
OF RESURRECTION

Those who teach the existence of another god besides the God of the Jews have no intelligent answer to give in response to my criticisms. True, they take as their defense the notion that the prophets of the Jews foretold the Christian God. But this is a very old ploy: those who offer up a new god really have none to give; and those who maintain that the prophets spoke of the God of the Jews and not about some other, better god will always come back with, "Yes, it was inevitable that things should have turned out the way they did—and why? Well, because it was predicted that they would." It is easy for the Christians to use the books of the Jews to their advantage, since anyone can prove anything from so-called prophecy: The predictions of the Pythian priestess, or of the priestesses of Dodona, or of the Clarian Apollo, or at Branchidae, or at the shrines of Zeus, Ammon, and of countless other prophets, the Christians regard as so much babble; but the predictions of the Judaean prophets, whether they were predictions or not, since those who live around Phoenicia and Palestine are used to speaking in a certain way, are taught as the unchanging word of God—as something wholly marvelous! Of this I have first-hand knowledge, knowing the people of that region as I do, and knowing the several types of prophecy.

For example, there are countless in that region who will "prophesy" at the drop of a hat, in or out of the temples. Others go about begging and claim to be oracles of God, plying their trade in the cities or in military outposts. They make a show of being "inspired" to utter their predictions.[172] These habitually claim to be more than prophets, and say such things as "I am God," or "I am a son of God," or even "I am the Holy Spirit," and "I have come [to bring life] for the world is coming to an end as I speak.

And the wicked will perish [in the fire] for their sins. I shall save you; you will yet see me, for I am coming again armed with heavenly powers. So blessed is he who worships me now. Those who refuse, whole cities and nations, will be cast into the fiery pit. Pity those who don't know me and what is ahead for them, for they will repent in vain and cry for mercy in vain. Those who hear me and believe in me will be saved (from the fire)." This sort of thing is heard all over Judaea by these most trivial of prophets; and they go on, after parading these threats in front of an audience, to babble about the signs of the Last Days—or to speak of mysterious happenings that no sane and intelligent person would trouble himself to figure out. Their talk is complete nonsense, and for this reason is appealing to the minds of fools and sorcerers, who can take their "predictions" and do with them what they like.

Indeed, I have talked with any number of these prophets after hearing them, and questioned them closely. On careful questioning (after gaining their confidence) they admitted to me that they were nothing but frauds, and that they concocted their words to suit their audiences and deliberately made them obscure.

Now it stands to reason that when the Christians point to the Jewish prophets in order to defend their doctrine of Christ, they are on very shaky ground indeed. To prove that God would suffer all sorts of indignities is no truer just because some Christian claims it was foretold in prophecy; for God does not suffer, and God cannot be humiliated; he does not call the wicked alone to be saved. A god would not eat the flesh of sheep (at Passover); a god would not drink vinegar and gall; a god does not filthy himself as the Christians say their Christ did. Look closely at their logic: If the prophets had said that the supreme God was to be born in servitude, that he would undergo a painful death as a slave, does this mean—given that it was foretold—that God must die such a death in order that through meeting the terms of the prophecy it might be believed that he was God? At any rate, this seems to be the run of their argument. But it does a foul injustice to the prophets, who could never have predicted such a thing. It is a perfidious misreading of the oracles of the Jews. So the question of whether they did or didn't predict the suffering and death of God does not count for anything. All that an intelligent person must ask himself is this: Do such claims do justice to the idea of God, since it is an axiom that what God does is good and that God does no act that is unworthy of his nature? This entails that what is disgraceful, mean, and unworthy should be disbelieved about God, no matter how many babbling fools say it was postulated of him. (For who are we to believe—a rabble of mistaken prophets, or the philosophers?)

It is mere impiousness, therefore, to suggest that the things that were done to Jesus were done to God. Certain things are simply as a matter of logic impossible to God, namely those things which violate the consistency of his nature: God cannot do less than what it befits God to do, what it is God's nature to do. Even if the prophets had foretold such things about the Son of God, it would be necessary to say, according to the axiom I have cited, that the prophets were wrong, rather than to believe that God has suffered and died.

I ask the Christians to consider further the following case: If the prophets of Yahweh, God of the Jews, were in the habit of telling the Jews that Jesus was to be his son, then why did he give them their laws through Moses and promise them that they would become rich and famous and fill the earth?[173] Why did he guarantee that they would slaughter their enemies (infants and all), and whole races of people, as Moses teaches, before their eyes?[174] Does he not threaten to do to them what he has done to their enemies for their disobedience?[175] Yet we are to believe that his "son," this man from Nazareth, gives an opposing set of laws: he says that a man cannot serve God properly if he is rich and famous or powerful[176] (or for that matter, if he is intelligent and reputable!). The Jews base their religion on God's promise to give them a land of plenty, but the Christians say one must pay no attention to food, or to one's larder—any more than the birds do— or to one's clothing, any more than the lilies do.[177] The Jews teach God's vengeance on their enemies, but Jesus advises that someone who has been struck should volunteer to be hit again. Well, who is to be disbelieved—Moses or Jesus? Perhaps there is a simpler solution: perhaps when the Father sent Jesus he had forgotten the commandments he gave to Moses, and inadvertantly condemned his own laws, or perhaps sent his messenger to give notice that he had suspended what he had previously endorsed.

What do the Christians suppose happens after death? Given that they represent God as having a body like our own, it is not surprising to find them saying that we go to another earth, different and better than this one. The latter notion they derive from the ancients, who taught that there is a happy life for the blessed—variously called the Isles of the Blessed, the Elysian fields—where they are free from the evils of the world. As Homer says, "The gods will take you to the Elysian plains at the ends of the earth, and there life will be easy."[178] Plato, who teaches the immortality of the soul, calls the place where the souls are sent a region: "The world is enormous, and our part of it, from the Pillars of Hercules to the Phasis, is only a fraction; like so many ants or frogs around a marsh, we mortals cluster about the sea, as do people elsewhere. And in various places around the earth there are hollows of differing sizes and shapes into which water, mist, and air have coalesced. But the land of the souls is pure and lies in the ethereal regions."[179] Plato's words are, to be sure, difficult; one cannot know for certain what he means when he says that because of our weakness and slowness we cannot get to the ethereal regions that lie atop the heavens, or when he says that only if we were able to bear the vision would we know true heaven and the true light when we saw it.

It seems that the Christians, in attempting to answer the question of how we shall know and see God, have misunderstood Plato's doctrine of reincarnation, and believe in the absurd theory that the corporeal body will be raised and reconstituted by God, and that somehow they will actually see God with their mortal eyes and hear him with their ears and be able to touch him with their hands. Such ideas can also be found among the hero cults of Trophinus, Amphiarus and Mopsus,[180] where it is claimed that gods may be seen in human form. [These, however, are not the supreme God] but men who were human in form and manifested their powers openly—not coming down secretly like this fellow who deceived the Christians in one virtually unnoticed apparition.

The Christians are preoccupied with the question of knowing God, and they think one cannot know God except through the senses of the body.[181] Thus they think not as men or souls think, but as the flesh thinks.[182] Still, I would try to teach them something, slow-witted though they are: If one shuts his eyes to the things of the senses and tries to see with his mind's eye, and if one turns from the flesh to the inner self, the soul, there he will see God and know God. But to begin the journey, you must flee from deceivers and magicians who parade fantasies in front of you. You will be a laughingstock so long as you repeat the blasphemy that the gods of other men are idols, while you brazenly worship as God a man whose life was wretched, who is known to have died (in disgraceful circumstances), and who, so you teach, is the very model of the God we should look to as our Father. The deceit you perpetrate with your ravings about miraculous doings, lions and other animals in double form, and superhuman doorkeepers (whose names you take the trouble to memorize!)[183] and the general madness of your beliefs, are to blame for the fact that you are marked for crucifixion. It is your rejection of true wisdom—that of inspired poets, wise men, philosophers, and the like—that [leads you to execution].

Plato teaches us the true theology when he writes, "To find the Maker and father of this universe is difficult; but it is impossible, having found him, to proclaim him to all men."[184] Both prophets and philosophers have sought the way of truth; but Plato knew that most men could not follow it. The wise men who speak of such things tell us that any conception of the Nameless First Being is dependent on proper reasoning—either on knowing his manifestations in the synthesis of things, by analyzing his distinction from the material world, or by analogy. In short, to talk about God is fraught with difficulty, because it is to talk about what is indescribable; and of this I would teach you, were you able to grasp it. But seeing that you are given to talking about the flesh and what happens to it, I doubt you would understand my lesson. Still:

Being and becoming are, in turn, intelligible and visible. Truth is inherent in being; error inherent in becoming. Knowledge has to do with truth, opinion with the other; and similarly, thought is concerned with what is intelligible, and sight with what is visible. Thus the mind knows what is intelligible, and the eye what is visible. What the sun is to visible things (as being neither the eye nor the sight, but rather the cause of the eye's vision, the existence of sight, the possibility of seeing visible things, and in turn the cause of objects' being made accessible to the senses), so is God to intelligible things.[185] He is not mind, intelligence, or knowledge; but he causes the mind to think, and is hence the cause of the existence of intelligence, the possibility of knowledge; he causes the existence of intelligible things—of truth itself, of being itself—since he transcends all things and is intelligible only by a certain power which cannot itself be described.

What I have just said, I have said to those able to understand it. You Christians would be doing well to understand any portion of it. And if any divine spirit had come down to preach divine truths about God, that spirit would have preached no other lesson. It was because that spirit operated even among the ancients that they were able to provide so many valuable instructions [for our benefit]. If you are not able to grasp their lessons, then keep quiet and cover your ignorance; do not try to tell us that those who can see are blind and that those who can run are really crippled, since it is you who are blind of spirit and crippled of soul, teaching a doctrine that relates only to the body and living in the hope of raising a dead thing to life. It would have been better had you in your zest for a new teaching formed your religion around one of the men of old who died a hero's death and was honored for it—someone who at least was already the subject of a myth. You could have chosen Herakles or Asclepios, or if these were too tame, there was always Orpheus, who, as everyone knows, was good and holy and yet died a violent death. Or had he already been taken? Well, then you had Anaxarchus, a man who looked death right in the eye when being beaten and said to his persecutors after being thrown into the mortar: "Beat away; beat the pouch of Anaxarchus; for it is not him you are beating."[186] But I recall that some philosophers have already claimed him as their master. Well, what of Epictetus? When his master was twisting his leg he smiled and said with complete composure, "You are breaking it." And when it was broken, he smiled and said, "I told you so."[187] Your God should have uttered such a saying when he was being punished![188] You would even get more credit if you had put forward the Sibyl (whom some among you cite anyway) as a child of God. Instead, you take her oracles and twist them,[189] inserting things to suit your purposes, including the notion that a man who lived a bad life and died a bad death was a god. You might even have chosen Jonah instead of Jesus—or Daniel, who escaped from the wild beasts, or those about whom similar fables are told.

You Christians have a saying that goes something like this: "Don't resist a man who insults you; even if he strikes you, offer him your other cheek as well."[190] This is nothing new, and it's been better said by others, especially by Plato, who ascribes the following to Socrates in the Crito:

"Then we should never do wrong?"

"Never."

"And should we not even try to avenge a wrong if we are wronged ourselves, as most would do, on the premise that we should never do wrong?"

"So it seems."

"So, should we do harm, Crito, or not?"

"I should say not, Socrates."

"Well, then, is it just or unjust to repay injury with injury?"

"Unjust, I would think."

"Because doing harm to men is no different from doing wrong?"

"Exactly so."

"So we should never take revenge and never hurt anyone even if we have been hurt.[191]

Thus writes Plato, and he continues:

"Be careful to see whether you agree with me and it is acceptable to you, and then let's reason together on the assumption that it is never right to do wrong and never right to take revenge; nor is it right to give evil for evil, or in the case of one who has suffered some injury, to attempt to get even. Do you agree with my premises or not? It seems to me the truth of what I say is evident, and seems as valid today as it did yesterday."[192]

This was Plato's opinion, and as he says, it was not new to
him but was pronounced by inspired men long before
him. What I have said about it may serve, part for whole,
as an example of the sorts of ideas the Christians mutilate.
But unless it is assumed that this is the only case, I assure
you that anyone who cares to try will find countless other
instances of their perversions of the truth: They say they
detest altars and images; so do the Scythians; so do the
nomads of Libya; so do the Seres, who don't believe in
God at all; and so do many everywhere, who have no use
for what is right. Herodotus tells us that the Persians take
the same view: "The Persians," he relates, "do not consider it legal to establish altars and images and temples; and
they think people who establish them are stupid. This idea
of theirs seems to come from the fact that they do not
regard the gods as having a nature similar to that of
human beings, as do the Greeks."[193] And Heracleitus con-
firms this when he writes, "They pray to images as if one
were to have a conversation with a house, having no idea
of the nature of gods and heroes."[194] Heracleitus, than
whom none is wiser, says rather secretively that it is
ridiculous to pray to images if one has no understanding
of the nature of gods and heroes. Further, Heracleitus may
be taken to mean that an image of stone, wood, bronze, or
gold, made by a craftsman, cannot be a god, and hence the
practice of praying to it is ludicrous. I mean, only a child
thinks that things are gods and not images of gods. But if
they mean that we should not worship images as divine
because God has a different shape, as the Persians seem to
think, then the Christians refute themselves: they teach,
do they not, that God made man in his own image, and
thus man's form is like his own. What sense is there, then,
to their refusal: if they will agree that images and votive
offerings are intended for the honor of certain beings
(whether they resemble these beings in form or not), why
maintain that those to whom they are dedicated are not

gods but demons, and then conclude that image worship is demon worship and not to be tolerated by the God-worshipers!

X. CHRISTIAN ICONOCLASM

Whatever the outcome of the debate over the form of God and the importance of images, the Christians are the losers, since they worship neither a god nor even a demon, but a dead man! Moreover, why should we not worship gods? I mean, if it is accepted that all of nature—everything in the world—operates according to the will of God and that nothing works contrary to his purposes, then it must also be accepted that the angels, the demons, heroes—everything in the universe—are subject to the will of the great God who rules over all. Over each sphere there is a being charged with the task of governance and worthy to have power, at least the power allotted it for carrying out its task. This being the case, it would be appropriate for each man who worships God also to honor the being who exercises his allotted responsibilities at God's pleasure, since that being must have been licensed to do what he does by God. Your Jesus says "It is impossible for the same man to serve many masters"[195] (and thus makes it appear that beings exist who exercise control quite apart from the will of God; but such a being would not be the great God at all, but some lower power). The notion that one cannot serve many masters is the sort of thing one would expect of the race of Christians—an eccentric position, but one perhaps predictable of a people who have cut themselves off from the rest of civilization. In so saying, they are really attributing their own feelings to God; for in the ordinary course of affairs, a man who is serving one master cannot really serve a second, since the first might be harmed by the man's loyalty to the second.

A man committed to one master could not pledge himself to a second, since in doing so he would be doing the one harm. It is perhaps equally reasonable, they would say, not to serve different heroes or demons at the same time. But God is not a man that he should be talked about as a "master." Harm, necessity, and sorrow are irrelevant where God is concerned: he is unaffected by injury, grief, and need. Thus it cannot be irrational to worship several gods; and the man who does so will naturally be worshiping some gods who derive from that greatest God, and will be loved for it. A man who honors what belongs to God does not offend God, since all belongs to him.[196]

Now, if the Christians worshiped only one God they might have reason on their side. But as a matter of fact they worship a man who appeared only recently.[197] They do not consider what they are doing a breach of monotheism; rather, they think it perfectly consistent to worship the great God and to worship his servant as God. And their worship of this Jesus is the more outrageous because they refuse to listen to any talk about God, the father of all, unless it includes some reference to Jesus: Tell them that Jesus, the author of the Christian insurrection, was not his son, and they will not listen to you. And when they call him Son of God, they are not really paying homage to God, rather, they are attempting to exalt Jesus to the heights.[198]

To prove my point I quote from their own book: In one of the divine dialogues, they say the following: " 'If the Son of God is mightier and the Son of Man is his Lord (and who will overcome the mighty God?) then how can it be that so many have seen the well but have not drunk from it? Why, having come to the end of your journey are you afraid?'—'You are wrong, for I have courage and a sword' "[199] Thus it is not their object to worship the almighty God, but the one whom they claim to be the father of Jesus, the cult fixture of their little society. They worship only this Son of Man, on the pretext that he is really a great god. And they say further that he is mightier than the lord of the almighty God. It was from this that they took their notion of not serving two masters, trying to ensure that [Jesus] would be preserved as the god and lord of the cult, unrivaled by any other.

The Christians abstain therefore from setting up altars and images, thinking that in doing so they are safeguarding the secrecy and obscurity of their little club. They think that in abstaining from things sacrificed to the gods they are preserving their sanctity. But to think in such a way is to cheapen the very idea of God, who belongs not to the Christians but to all men, and who—as he is perfectly good—needs no sacrifices anyway, as Plato somewhere says.[200] Such a god is not jealous for the devotion of particular people; necessity is foreign to his nature, and the homage people pay him has to do with their zeal, not his requirements. Understood in this way, there is nothing to prevent these Christians from participating in the public festivals in the spirit of social intercourse and as a sign of their fealty to the state. If, as they maintain, the idols are nothing, then there is nothing to prevent them from public-minded duties such as the festival.[201] On the other hand, if the idols are existent beings—demons of some sort, then they must belong to God himself, as he created all that exists; and if they occupy this position, it is a Christian's duty to pay them homage, to believe in them, sacrifice to them, and pray to them for the general good of the people.

But let us take their general point a further step: If they get their ideas from the spiritual fathers, the Jews, in not offering homage to the gods and in abstaining from certain animals, why do they not abstain from the flesh of all animals? Pythagoras, to name but one, refused to eat animal meat on the premise that he thereby honored the soul and its functions.[202] The Christians, however, take the view that they are abstaining from feasting with demons, and on this point I congratulate them: they acknowledge in so saying that they are always in the presence of the gods. I mean, of course, that although they avoid sacrifices they nonetheless breathe, eat, drink water and wine, and thus do not avoid the gods charged with the administration of each of these activities. So they are caught in the inconsistency of their own logic: either one ought not live at all—or else, having been born to live on this earth, we ought to give thanks to the gods who control earthly things, to render them the firstfruits and prayers, so that they will befriend us while we live. The wisest of the Greeks have said that even the human soul is allotted to gods from its birth; thus even we are to some extent under their control, and it is just as well if we do not slight them but rather do what we can to solicit their favor: The satraps or subordinate officers, not to mention the procurators who represent the Persian or Roman emperor—indeed even those who hold lesser offices—could make things very uncomfortable for anyone if they were slighted [as the Christians slight the gods]; and one should not expect the satraps and lieutenants of the earth and air to look kindly on the insults [of the new sect]. But of course they think otherwise: they assume that by pronouncing the name of their teacher they are armored against the powers of the earth and air[203] and that their God will send armies to protect them. And they teach that no demon, lest it be an evil one, could want to do them harm anyway. And they are quite insistent on the efficacy of the name as a means of protection: pronounce it improperly, they say, and it is ineffective. Greek and Latin will not do; it must be said in a barbarian tongue to work.

Silly as they are, one finds them standing next to a statue of Zeus or Apollo or some other god, and shouting, "See here: I blaspheme it and strike it, but it is powerless against me for I am a Christian!"[204] Does this good Chris-

tian fellow not see that I might do the same without fear of
reprisal to an image of his god? And further: those who do
stand next to your little god are hardly secure! You are
banished from land and sea, bound and punished for your
devotion to [your Christian demon] and taken away to be
crucified. Where then is your God's vengeance on his persecutors? Protection indeed!

You ridicule the images of the gods; I doubt you would
be so brave were you to come face to face with Herakles or
Dionysus himself; but that is hardly my point. I would call
your attention to the well-known fact that the men who
tortured your god in person suffered nothing in return;
not then, nor as long as they lived.[205] And what new
developments have taken place since your story proved
false—something that would encourage someone to think
that this man was not a sorcerer but the son of God? What
are we to think of a god so negligent that he not only
permitted his son to suffer as cruel a death as this Jesus
did, but who allowed the message he was sent to deliver
to perish with him? A long time has passed since then,
and nothing has changed.[206] Is there any human father so
ruthless as your god? You answer, "It is God's will that
things should happen as they happened."[207] And this is,
as I have said, your answer to everything: he subjected
himself to humiliation because it was his will to be humiliated. I would be negligent indeed if I did not suggest that
the gods you blaspheme might say it was *their* will, and
better sense would come of the episode if I did. Or one
could say that anytime a god is blasphemed he endures it,
and that endurance alone does not prove someone a god:
one endures unalterable situations as much out of necessity as by choice. Who is to say necessity is not to be reckoned in the case of Jesus? When one considers these
things objectively, it is evident that the old gods are rather
more effective in punishing blasphemers than is the god of
the Christians, and those who blaspheme the former are

usually caught and punished: just how effective is the Christian god in that respect?

Certainly the Christians are not alone in claiming inspiration for the utterances they ascribe to their god through their prophets. I need hardly mention every case of prophecy that is said to have occurred among our own people—prophets and prophetesses as well, both men and women, claiming the power of oracular and inspired utterance. What of those who have claimed the power to discern truth, using victims and sacrifices of one kind and another, and those who say that they are privy to certain signs or gifts given to them by the powers that be? Life is full of such claims: Cities have been built because a prophet says, "Build it!"; Diseases and famines have been dealt with in their oracles, and those who neglected their advisories have often done so at their peril. The prophets have foretold disaster with some accuracy; colonists have heeded their warnings before going to foreign parts, and have fared the better for it; not common people alone, but rulers have paid attention to what they have to say; the childless have gotten their hearts' desire and have escaped the curse of loneliness because prophets have helped them; ailments have been healed. On the other hand, how many have insulted the temples and been caught? Some have been overcome with madness as soon as they blasphemed; others have confessed their wrongdoing; others have been moved to suicide; others have been punished with incurable diseases; some have been destroyed by a voice coming from within the shrine itself! Are these distinctive happenings unique to the Christians—and if so, how are they unique? Or are ours to be accounted myths and theirs believed? What reasons do the Christians give for the distinctiveness of their beliefs?

In truth there is nothing at all unusual about what the Christians believe, except that they believe it to the exclusion of more comprehensive truths about God. They believe in eternal punishment; well, so do the priests and initiates of the various religions. The Christians threaten others with this punishment, just as they are themselves threatened. To decide which of the two threats is nearer the truth is fairly simple; but when confronted with the evidence, the Christians point to the evidence of miracles and prophecies that they think bolsters their case.

There is no disguising the absurdity of the Christian view when it comes to reward and punishment, however. For on the one hand they yearn for the restoration of their earthly body (as if there were nothing better than that to salvage!) in just the same form as it appeared during a man's life. On the other hand, they prescribe casting the bodies of all those who discredit them into hell, as if the body were of no value at all. But there is no use in dwelling on this point, especially with a group of people so thoroughly bound to flesh-and-blood concerns. Such people are commonly boorish by nature, and not a little unsmart by most applicable standards; not only so, they are usually rebellious creatures at heart. I should be glad to make my point clear to those among them, if there are such, who would profit from hearing about how a soul or mind comes to reside eternally with God (whatever they want to call this—the psyche, or an intellectual spirit, a living soul, or a superrational and irreducible product of a divine and incorporeal nature). Perhaps it is sufficient to say that whoever leads a good life will be happy hereafter, and on this point even the Christians would have to agree. Those who are wicked will be afflicted with unhappiness eternally. This doctrine, however, is not theirs by origin: it is theirs by derivation, and it is one that neither they nor any person would wish to abandon.

Men are born in bodily form; they are bound to it; they are weighted down by the passions and needs of the world and are paying the penalty for their sins, until such time as the soul has been purified through its successive stages. As Empedocles teaches, "It [the soul] must wander about, away from the blessed, for thirty thousand years, becoming in its time every possible shape of mortal being."[208] The soul is guarded in the here and now by the wardens of our earthly prison. This is in the nature of our mortal existence: we are given to gatekeepers for purposes ordained by God; the gatekeepers do their duty at God's pleasure. It makes little sense, therefore, for the Christians to heap abuse on the officers, the demons, in charge of our prison. They offer their bodies to be tortured and killed to no purpose when they think that in so doing they are defying the demons and going to their eternal reward. They have carried to an extreme a principle that we revered first: namely, that it does no one any good, in the end, to love life inordinately. But to hate life is just as wicked. The Christians do not suffer for a principle but because they break the law; they are not martyrs but robbers.[209]

Reason requires one of two things: If they persist in refusing to worship the various gods who preside over the day-to-day activities of life, then they should not be permitted to live until marriageable age; they should not be permitted to marry, to have children, nor to do anything else over which a god presides. If they are going to marry, have children and have a good time of it, taking the bad with the good as all men must,[210] then they ought to pray to the beings who have made life possible for them. They should offer the appropriate sacrifices and say the proper prayers until such time as they are free of their earthly entanglements, and ingratiate themselves to the beings who control all spheres of human activity. It is at best ungrateful to use someone's flat and pay them no rent (as Christians do the earth).

That life is under the control of gods one can see from the writings of the Egyptians.[211] They say that a man's body is under the power of thirty-six demons (or gods of some sort) who divide it among themselves, one for each part of the body. The demons are known under various names: Chnoumen, Chnachoumen, Knat, Sikat, Biou, Erou, Erebiou, Rhamanoor, Rheianoor, and all the other names that they use in their language. By invoking these names, they heal the appropriate part of the body. In any case, what is to prevent someone from paying homage to these and to the other gods, if he so chooses—so that at least one can be healthy and not ill, have good luck rather than bad, and be delivered from misfortunes of all sorts. Instead the Christians make ridiculous claims for themselves: "At the name of Jesus every knee in heaven and earth, and those under the earth, and every tongue confesses Jesus is Lord."[212] I am not making the case for invoking demons, however; I am merely trying to show that the Christians do the same things that the Egyptians do in memorizing the names of thirty-six different demons, only they choose to invoke but one. One must be careful about believing such things lest one become so engrossed in healing, and lapse into the superstitions associated with the magical arts, that one is turned aside from the higher things, the appropriate objects of reflection. Some skeptics say—and perhaps we should believe them—that the demon is part and parcel of the things created by God, and is riveted to blood and burnt offerings and magical enchantments, and the like. Healing and predicting the future are their sphere, but their knowledge and activity concern only mortal activities. This being so, it is well to acknowledge the demons formally only when reason dictates, and reason may not dictate our doing so in every case. It is perhaps better to think that the demons require nothing, long for nothing, demand nothing. They may be pleased with our little tokens of recognition, but what ought really to occupy our minds, day and night, is the Good: publicly and privately, in every word and deed and in the silence of reflection, we should direct ourselves toward the con-

templation of the Good. So long as God is the subject of
our thoughts, the little devotions we perform on behalf of
the powers of this world—not the demons only but the
rulers and princes who hold power at the gods' design—
are surely nothing horrible. Indeed, it is only insanity for
the Christians to refuse their religious duties, rushing
headlong to offend the emperor and the governors and to
invite their wrath. To love the emperor and to serve God
are complementary duties:[213] if one worships God, he will
not be influenced by those who command him to utter
blasphemies or to whisper seditious things about the au-
thorities. One would rather die than say or think anything
profane about God: one remains firm. But on this logic, is
not the Christian rejection of the gods blasphemy even
against the God they profess to worship? For if we are
commanded to worship the great god Helios or to speak
well of Athena, we are in so doing worshiping God as
well; so in singing a hymn to Mithra or to Athena, the
Christians would at least not seem to be atheists,[214] but
would be seen as believers in the great God. The worship
of God is only magnified in the worship of the gods.

So too: If someone says to a Christian, "Here, I command you swear by the emperor," that is nothing to be
feared. You are swearing by the man to whom all earthly
power has been given: what you receive in life, you receive from him. (And that is what it means to be a god.) It
is not wise to disbelieve the ancient sage who said "Let
there be one king: one to whom the crafty Kronos gave the
power."[215] Overturn this axiom and you will know how
swiftly punishment can be dealt! If everyone were to
adopt the Christian's attitude, moreover, there would be
no rule of law: the legitimate authority would be abandoned; earthly things would return to chaos and come
into the hands of the lawless and savage barbarians; and
nothing further would be heard of Christian worship or of
wisdom, anywhere in the world. (Indeed, even for your

superstition to persist, the power of the emperor is necessary.) Or would you suggest that if the Romans could be persuaded by you and we were to give up our laws and customs and call on the name of your Most High God (whatever name you choose for him) to come and fight on our side we would no longer have need for a military defense? Would your God preserve the empire? You are fond of saying that in the old days this same Most High God made these and greater promises to those who gave heed to his commandments and worshiped him. But at the risk of appearing unkind, I ask how much good those promises have done either the Jews before you or you in your present circumstances. And would you have us put our faith in such a god? Instead of being masters of the whole world, the Jews have today no home of any kind. In your case, if anyone professes your odd beliefs, he must do so in secret, or else be hounded and finally delivered for trial and condemned to death.

You are really quite tedious in your claims: If those who now reign were persuaded by your doctrines, you argue, and these same were taken prisoner, you could persuade those who reign after them and those after and so on and so on, more and more reigning and being taken captive and the like, until there came finally a ruler who, being sensible and reading these events as representing the will and plan of God, would try wiping you out before you succeeded in bringing down the empire and him with it. Ah, that it were possible for there to be one law for the whole world—to bring Asia, Europe, Libya, Greeks and barbarians and all alike, under one roof, so to speak. But to wish for this is to wish for nothing. We are citizens of a particular empire with a particular set of laws, and it behooves the Christians at least to recognize their duties within the present context: namely, to help the emperor in his mission to provide for the common good; to cooperate with him in what is right and to fight for him if it becomes necessary, as though we were all soldiers or fellow generals. This is what a good man does: he accepts public office for the preservation of the law and of religion, if it becomes necessary for him to do so; he does not run from public duty. He does not defile the appointed laws, on the [premise that if everyone did so, it would not be possible for the law to function at all].

So much for the doctrines of the Christians. It remains for me now to compose another treatise, for the profit of those willing and able to believe what I have said here, and to teach them how to lead a good life.

CELSUS

NOTES

1. Celsus may here refer to the so-called *institutum Neronianum*, mentioned by Tertullian (*Ad nationes* 1.7; *Apology* 5) and Sulpicius Severus (*Chronicles* 2.29). Hardening attitudes toward the Christian cultus in Rome in the final decades of the first century are also evident from Suetonius' testimony (*The Twelve Caesars*, 16; 25.4) and that of Tacitus (*Annals* 15.44). Not until the beginning of the third century was there an enactment binding throughout the Empire proscribing Christianity. In the second century, the profession of the Christian faith was dealt with by the process known as *cognitio*, in which provincial magistrates had unlimited discretionary powers. The Emperor Trajan's letter to the younger Pliny, proconsul of Pontus-Bythinia, in 111, suggests that the general tendency of the time was to be lenient with those who adhered to the new religion. See A. N. Sherwin-White, "The Early Persecution and the Roman Law, Again," *Journal of Theological Studies*, 3 (1952), 199.

2. Fragment 5; cf. Origen, *Against Celsus* 7.62, and note 6 below; Clement of Alexandria, *Exhortation*, 4.50.4. Celsus here attempts to show that the Christian aversion to images is a derivative doctrine; Origen (1.5–6) argues that Christian practice reflects the perfection of a moral principle "written by God in the hearts of men." Both Origen and Celsus regard iconoclasm as an ethical question: The Christians are guilty of breaching tradition and thus deserve to be treated as outlaws.

3. Cf. Acts 3.5f; 5.15; 8.4–8. According to the longer ending of Mark's gospel (16.9–20, not in the most ancient manuscripts) Jesus authorized the disciples to exorcise, heal, and perform miracles in his name. That the early Christian mission was advanced by the use of magic is well attested; see Morton Smith, *Jesus the Magician* (New York, 1978).

4. The source of Celsus' suggestion is not clear; his accusation may reflect a misreading of Mark 13.22 or of the rebukes of the apostles (Mark 8.17ff.; 21, 33). Mark 14.50–51 points to an early tradition con-

cerning the desertion of the whole company of apostles, at the end of a section that includes Judas' betrayal (14.10) and the prediction of Peter's denials (14.26). Whatever gospel Celsus possessed—conceivably a Marcionite text—must have emphasized the related traditions of rebuke and desertion. Cf. Origen, *Against Celsus*, 2.39.

5. The nucleus of Celsus' complaint is that Christianity is just another instance of the irrationality that characterizes the mystery cults. Galen (ca. 130–200) also knows Christianity as a cult that promotes superstition and exploits the gullibility of the poor and illiterate by "ordering [its pupils] to accept everything on faith" (cf. Richard Walzer, *Galen on Jews and Christians* [London, 1949], p. 15).

6. In the gospels, the emphasis on simplicity appears in such passages as Mark 10.15f. and Luke 10.21; in Paul's letters, I Cor. 2.1f. and 1.18–22 appear to reflect the typical Christian attitude of the time—the middle decades of the first century—toward wisdom, defined as book-learning and facility of speech in oral argumentation (cf. I Cor. 1.17–20). It is the refusal of the Christians to test their doctrines in open debate that Celsus finds irritating; Origen, in responding to the complaint, does not take exception to the characterization as such: "With respect to the business of 'faith' which you speak of so frequently: we consider [faith] a useful thing for the masses; and it is true that those who have no way of abandoning their livelihood in order to learn philosophy we instruct to believe without examining the reasons for their belief" (*Against Celsus*, 1.10).

7. Celsus' encyclopaedic survey is designed to show that the doctrines of Christianity, being derived from Judaism, are inadequate to the same extent that Judaism is inadequate. A frequent criticism of Christianity in the second century was its novelty—a criticism from which earlier missionaries like Paul seem to have derived encouragement (I Cor. 2.24), but apologists like Justin Martyr (ca. 160) found it more profitable to represent Christianity as the revelation of eternally true doctrines adumbrated in Judaism and pagan philosophy (1 *Apology* 32; 59) Origen argues (1.18) that none of the writings cited by Celsus is extant, and that in any event they would not bear comparison with the Mosaic history.

8. Celsus refers to Critias' tale in the *Timaeus* (22): "Once upon a time, Phaeton, the son of Helios, having yoked the steeds in his father's chariot because he was not able to drive them up the path of his father, burnt up all that was on the earth. . . . Now this has the form of a myth, but really signifies a declination of the bodies moving in the heavens around the earth and a great conflagration of things upon the earth which recurs after long intervals." The resolution of this catastro-

phe is achieved by a periodic world deluge, sent by the gods to purge the earth. Two are spared, Deucalion and Pyrrha. Celsus' high regard for Egyptian wisdom (*Against Celsus*, 1.14; 6.80) leads him to conclude that the Hebrew myth is secondary.

9. On Egyptian circumcision, cf. Herodotus, *History*, 2,104; Origen, *Homily on Jeremiah*, 5.14. As elsewhere, the argument here devolves into quibbling over who copied from whom: Origen (1.22) argues that the Egyptians make use of the name of Abraham in some of their magical formulas and began to circumcize in imitation of Jewish practice.

10. An elaborate hierarchy of angels is developed in the Old Testament pseudepigraphic books, notably in I Enoch 9–12, written in the second century B.C.E. The advocacy of angel worship is also charged against the heretics envisaged in Col. 2.18, where it is linked to certain practices of self-mortification. Celsus assumes that Moses worked wonders in Egypt by having learned magical arts. See Smith, *Jesus the Magician*, pp. 21–70.

11. Cf. I Corinthians 2.6f.

12. Celsus doubtless has in mind such teachers as Ignatius of Antioch and Clement of Rome, whose typological interpretations of the Old Testament paved the way for the allegorical exegesis of Clement of Alexandria and Origen himself.

13. For analysis of the talmudic and midrashic traditions concerning the birth of Jesus and the miracles, see my *Jesus Outside the Gospels* (New York, 1984), 36–60. Celsus' allusion to these stories is important evidence for their currency in the second century; he may well know of written traditions, prevalent in Jewish circles, designed to refute the gospels.

14. The name "Panthera" is the common one for the Roman father of Jesus in the Jewish polemical literature. The story itself may suggest an attempt by the polemicists to discredit the Christian account of the virgin birth: "Panthera" (panther) may be a pun on the Greek word for virgin, *parthenos*, used in Matthew 1.23 to suggest that the birth of Jesus conformed to Old Testament prophecy (Isa. 7.14).

15. It was a convention in Jewish circles that Jesus did his miracles by magical arts learned in Egypt, an allegation that seems to be at issue in such apologetic sections of the gospels as Mark 3.22–23. In the *Tol'doth Yeshu*, a compendium of tales based on talmudic and midrashic traditions, Jesus is depicted as one who learned spells in Egypt and returned to Jerusalem where he "led Israel astray" by his craft. See further my *Jesus Outside the Gospels*, pp. 46–50.

16. On the classical analogues of the synoptic infancy narratives,

see the material given in Dungan, *Sources for the Study of the Gospel* (Philadelphia, Pa., 1980), pp. 129–36.

17. Smith, *Jesus the Magician*, p. 96f., has located an interesting parallel to the epiphany story of Mark 1.11 in a Greek magical papyrus.

18. Cf. I John 3.1.

19. The story is unique to Matthew (2.9f.), though it is not known whether Celsus would have known the text of Matthew's gospel. On the identification of the Chaldeans, see J. Bidez and Franz Cumont, *Les Mages hellenisés* (Paris, 1938), pp. i, 33–36.

20. Whether Celsus misrepresents the number of apostles deliberately—perhaps to deprecate the symbolic significance of the twelve—or is unaware of the precise number cannot be determined. In Jewish polemic, Jesus is reckoned to have had fewer apostles than the gospels suggest. Luke 10.1ff. seems designed to counter the charge that Jesus was unable to attract large numbers of followers (cf. Mark 6.7).

21. Matt. 2.13ff.; the material cited is peculiar to Matthew's gospel.

22. Celsus seems to have in mind John 10.24.

23. Mark 6.34–44.

24. Cf. Apuleius, *Metamorphoses*, 1.4. Celsus regards the disciples as garden variety magicians who hawk their wares in the marketplace (Acts 5.12–16).

25. Luke 24.43. The passage in Luke seems contrived to offer irrefragable proof of the physical resurrection of Jesus. Its apologetic purpose is now well established, having been designed to combat certain docetic heresies (as for example those of Marcion and Basilides) which maintained that Jesus was a human being in appearance only. See my *Marcion: On the Restitution of Christianity* (Chico, Calif., 1984), pp. 155–83, esp. pp. 119–24.

26. Jewish responsibility in the actual execution of Jesus is a curious feature of Celsus' polemic; he seems to accept the familiar Talmudic tradition that Jesus was stoned, then hung up for display, on the eve of Passover—a tradition still to be discerned in I Thess. 2.15. Cf. Hoffmann, *Jesus Outside the Gospels*, pp. 48–49.

27. Celsus is strangely modern in making this distinction between the historical Jesus and the beliefs of the disciples. Cf. Mark 14.12.

28. Celsus argues that if Jesus was a god he had an obligation to make himself known in word and deed; passages such as Mark 3.13, suggesting a certain reluctance on Jesus' part to promote his reputation as a healer, are taken to mean that Jesus did not wish to be regarded as a god. It is now commonly recognized that these passages (cf. Mark 6.43, 8.36, etc.) are a feature of the dramatic irony of Mark's gospel. On

the subject of "secrecy" as a theme in the gospels, see Wilhelm Wrede, *The Messianic Secret* (Cambridge, 1971), pp. 24–81.

29. Here again, Celsus' literalism leads him to conclude that the agony in the garden of Gethsemane (Mark 14.32–42), which seems to have been designed (like Luke 24.43) to emphasize a particular church's christology—in this instance an antidocetic one—proves that Jesus lacked the essential theotic virtue of imperturbability. Mark 15, the trial before Pilate (not mentioned by Celsus) asserts that Jesus displayed the attitude expected of a god following his arrest.

30. Cf. Mark 14.17–21, 14.32f.; 14.66–72.

31. Mark 10.32–34; 9.29–31; 8.31–33.

32. An allusion to gnostic-docetic christologies. Celsus must certainly have known of Marcionite teaching (*Against Celsus*, 5.62) and shows some awareness of other sects which denied the physical suffering of Jesus on the cross. Most christologies of the early period were docetic to some degree (cf. John 20.19; Mark 16.12, 19). Celsus' argument centers on the philosophical incongruity in postulating suffering of a god.

33. Cf. John 2.24–25.

34. Mark 14.36, pars.

35. This charge is a familiar one: Marcionite teachers alleged that the apostles had falsified the gospels and in turn were accused by orthodox bishops of "mutilating" the gospels and letters of Paul. Cf. Irenaeus, *Against Heresies*, 3.12.12; Tertullian, *Against Marcion*, 4.2. It is not clear that the Marcionites knew of other gospels, and in any event they credited only a prototype version of Luke as being, according to their tradition, the gospel known and preached by Paul. On this, see my *Marcion: On the Restitution of Christianity*, pp. 142–45.

36. Chadwick (*Origen, Contra Celsum*, p. 93, note 3) notes that this passage shows "that Celsus is aware of the Logos-theology of hellenistic Judaism." Philo (*Husbandry*, 51; *On Languages*, 146) speaks of the Logos as the son of God.

37. Celsus seems here to refer to the Lucan genealogy (Luke 3.23–38) rather than to the Matthean list (Matt. 1.1–17), which begins with David.

38. In Euripides' *Bacchantes* (488–551) a trial scene reminiscent of that related in the synoptic gospels describes Dionysus' appearance before Pentheus. Challenged to reveal his godhead, Dionysus assures Pentheus that the god within will set him free at his pleasure; in the end, Pentheus is torn to pieces for failing to recognize Dionysus as a god. The point of Celsus' argument—that if Jesus had been a god his executioners would have suffered the fate of a Pentheus—was not

missed by later writers, such as the pseudonymous author of the "Letter of Pilate to Claudius" (Hoffmann, *Jesus Outside the Gospels*, p. 65f.).

39. Celsus here contrasts Jesus' cry from the cross (Mark 15.34) with the death cry of Alexander, who, when wounded, is said to have pointed to his blood and declared "This is not ichor." Cf. Plutarch, *Lives of the Noble Greeks and Romans*, 28; Seneca, *Epistles*, 59.12.

40. Cf. Eph. 2.13–17.

41. Mark 13.6f.

42. Herodotus, *History*, 4.95: "Zamolis . . . [taught his companions] that neither they nor any of their posterity would ever perish but that they would all go to a place where they would live forever, enjoying every possible good. While he [was thus speaking] he was constructing an apartment underground into which, when it was completed, he withdrew, vanishing suddenly from the eyes of the Thracians, who mourned his loss as one dead. He, meanwhile, stayed in his secret chamber three full years, after which he came forth from his concealment and showed himself once more to his countrymen, who were thus brought to believe in the truth of what he taught them."

43. Cf. Diogenes Laertius, *Lives of the Philosophers*, 8.41; Tertullian, *On the Soul*, 28.

44. Herodotus, *History*, 2.122. According to Herodotus, the priests once a year celebrated the descent of Rhampsinitus into Hades.

45. On the Orpheus myth, see W. H. C. Guthrie, *Orpheus and Greek Religion* (Cambridge, 1935), 29ff.

46. Apollodorus, *The Library*, 3.30–31.

47. Apollodorus, *The Library*, 2.5.12.

48. The earthquake is mentioned only by Matthew (27.45–54).

49. Celsus appears to have the account of John 20.1–18 in view, though the reference may be to another gospel of uncertain vintage. The tradition that the women rather than the disciples were the first witnesses of the resurrection is very ancient: in the original ending of Mark's gospel (16.8) they are known as the sole recipients of visions of the risen Jesus—a tradition which Celsus here seems to acknowledge.

50. On this theme in the gospels, see Wrede, *The Messianic Secret*, pp. 24–81.

51. Acts 8.51; cf. Peter's speech, Acts 4.8–12. Early Christian polemic implicated the Jews in the death of Jesus, but the synoptic gospels present Jesus as wishing to keep his identity a secret, thus responding, proleptically, to the failure of the Jews to acknowledge Jesus as Messiah. The themes of unresponsiveness and secrecy stand unreconciled in early Christian tradition; Celsus here comments on the inconsistency of the Christian position.

52. Cf. Matt. 11.20.

53. Plato, *Phaedrus*, 260C: a dispute of no importance.

54. Asclepios (Lat. Aesculapius) was believed to be the son of Apollo and Coronis. Having been taught the art of medicine by Cheiron the centaur, he restored Hippolytus to life at the behest of Artemis and was struck down by Zeus in reprisal. Asclepios was honored as the god of healing; his principle temple was at Epidaurus, but as Celsus rightly notes, the fame of the god was widespread in the hellenistic world, and some of the miracle stories in the gospels reflect a background in the legends associated with Asclepios.

55. Aristeas: According to legend, a servant of Apollo. Aristeas is reputed to have produced the semblance of death by effecting a literal separation of the soul from the body (*ecstasis*), appearing at the same moment elsewhere—sometimes in nonhuman shape. Cf. Mark 16.12. On Aristeas, see Herodotus, *History*, 4.13f.

Cleomedes: Mentioned by Plutarch (*Romulus* 28) as a trickster who had perfected a disappearing act. Celsus' allusion to Cleomedes is in line with his general contention that, as a magician, Jesus may have tricked his disciples into believing that he had conquered death.

56. Cf. Tertullian (on martyrdom among the Christians), *Apology*, 50: "Your cruelty, however exquisite, avails you nothing. Rather, it is a temptation for us. The oftener we are mown down by you, the more we grow.

57. Celsus here echoes a complaint also voiced by Justin in his 1 *Apology* (26): factions and dissension make it difficult for outsiders to determine precisely what Christians profess. Justin's argument is designed to suggest that true Christianity has been obscured by the false teachings of the heretics, especially the Marcionites. Celsus' point is that the factions can only have arisen because the new religion lacks a solid basis for its doctrines.

58. Cf. Lucian, *Imaginings*, 11; Clement of Alexandria, *The Pedagogue*, 3.4.

59. The comparison between the wonders of Asclepios and the miracles of Jesus is a standard feature of anti-Christian polemic: cf. F. G. Doelger, *Antike und Christentum* (Muenster, 1929–50), vol. 4, pp. 250–57.

60. Celsus has in mind a story taken from Pindar (Frag. 284) and Herodotus (*History* 4.14–15). According to Herodotus, Aristeas, having died, appeared in Cyzicus and Proconnesus after his death, and centuries later to the Metapontines, who were told to set up an altar to Apollo, and near it a statue dedicated to Aristeas.

61. Herodotus, *History*, 4.36. The story of Abaris is also known to Porphyry (*Pythagoras* 28–29) and Iamblichus (*Pythagoras* 19.91).

62. Chadwick has shown (*Origen, Contra Celsus*, 149) that Celsus' references are "stock miracle-stories which often occur together in similar groups elsewhere, e.g., Plutarch *Romulus*, 28 (Aristeas, Cleomedes); Pliny, *Natural History*, 7. 174–76, (Hermotimus, Aristeas, Epimenides, Heraclides' lifeless woman); Clement of Alexandria, *Miscellanies*, 1.133.2 (Abaris, Aristeas, Epimenides)," and so forth. The story of Hermotimus of Clazomenae, burned while asleep after boasting to his wife that his soul left his body at night, is related by Apollonius (*Mirabilia* 3) and Pliny (*Natural History* 7.174). Its use in anti-Christian polemic in known to Tertullian (*On the Soul* 44).

63. Plutarch, *Romulus*, 28.

64. Celsus here offers a list of oracles honored in various regions. Origen argues (3.35) that if Celsus "maintains that the persons he has named were demons, heroes, or gods [then] he has proved the very thing he does not want to accept: namely, that Jesus was a person of a similar nature."

65. Antinous was deified and the city of Antinoopolis founded by Hadrian in his memory, ca. 130 C.E. Cf. Dio Cassius 69.11.

66. But cf. Matt. 12.28 and John 15.1–5.

67. The social description of the Christian church bears comparison with Paul's words to the Corinthian church (I Cor. 6–9–11), the latter reflecting the composition of a church in the middle decades of the first century. The charge that Christianity exploits children seems to come from Celsus' reading of Mark 10.13–16, which he rightly interprets to refer to the condition of childlike simplicity necessary for the acceptance of Christian preaching.

68. Celsus testifies here to the Christian practice of healing by faith (cf. Acts 3.6) and the practice of advising Christians to avoid the medical arts.

69. It is uncertain whether Celsus would have known Paul's letters; the attitude he describes is certainly articulated in I Cor. 4.18ff., but the radical Paulinists of the second century seem to have been equally averse to learned dispute as a method of arriving at the truth of propositions. Apelles, a disciple of Marcion and thereafter head of his own Christian sect, exemplifies the position described by Celsus; cf. Eusebius, *Ecclesiastical History*, 5.13.5f.

70. The same criticism is voiced by Tertullian against the "unknown" God of the Marcionites: *Against Marcion* 1.22.2–3.

71. See Franz Cumont, *Lux Perpetua* (Paris, 1949), p. 219f.

72. II Peter 3.7; Eph. 6.16.

73. Celsus has in mind a number of texts: Plato, *Republic*, 381b,c and *Phaedrus*, 246d; also Lucretius 5.146; Diogenes Laertius 10.139: "A blessed and eternal being has no trouble himself and brings no trouble upon any other being; he is exempt from movements of anger and partiality" [Epicurus]; cf. Cicero, *On the Nature of the Gods,* 1.19.50f.

74. Celsus bases this dilemma on the two forms of Christianity with which he is best acquainted: God either undergoes a substantial change, contrary to the principle of immutability and thus impossible for a god, or else he appears to do so through deceit, which is equally contrary to the divine nature. The orthodox Logos christology, involving a physical incarnation of the divine principle (John 1.1–14) epitomizes the former; gnostic-docetic Christianity, especially that of the Sethian Gnostics (see *Second Treatise of the Great Seth* VII.2/56.21–27f.)., the latter.

75. Celsus apparently shares in common with the Marcionites a literalist reading of God's *metanoia* (repentance) in the Book of Genesis (6.6); cf. *Against Marcion* 1.16.4; 2.23.1.

76. Perhaps an echo of Eph. 2.1–22.

77. On the rival claims of the races, see Chadwick, 211, note 1. Josephus advances the argument in favor of Jewish antiquity as a defense of the religion of the Jews in the *Against Apion.*

78. Gen. 2.21f.

79, Gen. 3.21–23.

80. Gen. 7.11ff.

81. Celsus has in mind Gen. 18.17, where Sarah's age is reckoned to be ninety years at the time of the conception of Isaac. Cf. Luke 1.7, 18, 36.

82. Mentioned by a variety of church fathers, including Clement of Alexandria and Jerome, this dialogue is not extant. Cf. Eusebius, *Ecclesiastical History*, 4.6.3. The work was translated into Latin in Africa in the late third century.

83. The basis of Celsus' speculation at this point is the *Timaeus,* 69c,d: "Now of the divine, [God] was himself the creator, but the creation of the mortal, he committed to his offspring."

84. *Timaeus* 81d. Cf. Paul's discussion I Cor. 150 on "kinds" of flesh: "*Hoti sarx kai haima basileian theou klēronomēsai ou dynatai oude heā phthora tēn aphtharsian klēronomei*" ("Flesh and blood cannot inherit the kingdom of God, nor can corruption inherit incorruption").

85. This discussion seems to presuppose gnostic-Christian views concerning the increase in evil as a correlate of the continuing diremption of the pleroma in the created order. The Marcionites also believed

that the procreative order involved an increase in evil: Tertullian, *The Prescription*, 7 and *Against Marcion* 1.2.2; Epiphanius, *Panarion*, 24.6.

86. Origen (*Against Celsus* 4.63) cited Plotinus (*Enneads* 1.8.9) to the effect that evils are indeterminate in number and thus cannot be shown to increase or decrease.

87. Plato, *Republic*, 379C.

88. Plato, *Politics*, 269C, 270A.

89. Isa. 65.17ff., a prophecy central to the early Christian apocalyptists; cf. II Pet. 3.13; Rev. 21.4–5.

90. Celsus refers to the destruction of Jerusalem by the Roman forces under Titus in August of 70: the contrast he intends is between the power of Rome, manifested in the destruction of the Temple, and the powerlessness of the Christian God, which he claims is reflected in the killing of Jesus.

91. The subject here broached by Celsus is discussed by Martin Pohlenz, *Die Stoa* (Goettingen, 1948), vol. I, pp. 81ff.

92. Euripides, *Phoenician Maidens*, 546.

93. Pliny, *Natural History*, 11.110. What follows in this section Celsus takes from a variety of ancient writers.

94. Cf. Herodotus, *History*, 2.73.

95. Gen. 6.6–7.

96. It is not clear that Celsus knows Paul's discourse on the resurrection of the body in I Cor. 15.35–50. Tertullian (*Apology* 48; *On the Soul* 56; *On the Resurrection of the Flesh*, passim.) makes a distinction between the flesh to be raised and the material body, arguing along Pauline lines that the resurrection body is specially prepared for its destiny.

97. Cf. Tertullian, *On the Resurrection of the Flesh*, 48–49. Among the Jews, the Sadducees rejected the idea of bodily resurrection (Luke 20.27). Celsus bases his objection on the Platonic doctrine that the body is an encumbrance to the immortal soul.

98. Cf. John 14.12–14.

99. Heracleitus, Frag. 96. Cf. Plato, *Timaeus*, 37.

100. Cf. Plato, *Phaedrus*, 247.

101. Herodotus *History*, 2.18.

102. Celsus takes his information from books 1 and 3 of Herodotus.

103. Herodotus, *History*, 3.38.

104. Pindar, Frag. 152.

105. Herodotus, *History*, 1.131.

106. Celsus' complaint echoes certain gnostic criticisms of Moses' "sorcery" and deception, such as we find in the *Apocryphon of John* (II.1/22.21–25) and *Second Seth* (VII.2/63.26–64.22) from Nag Hammadi.

107. Celsus seems to have in view certain Christian interpretations

of Enoch 6–10 and 67–69. The Christians may have suggested that such punishment was reserved for "false" messiahs (Mark 13.6).

108. Celsus points out the well-known discrepancy in the resurrection accounts given by Mark (16.5: a single young man [*neaniskos*]) and Luke (24.4: two men [*andres duo*]).

109. Cf. Matt. 28.2.

110. This suggests that Celsus was well aware of the Matthean account of the nativity (Matt. 1.20; 2.12).

111. See my *Marcion: On the Restitution of Christianity* (1984), pp. 155–208, on the sources of Marcion's dualism. That Celsus knew of the Marcionites suggests the prominence of Marcionite Christianity in the closing decades of the second century. See, further, Justin, 1 *Apology*, 26.

112. Celsus may be referring to the Valentinian anthropology described by Irenaeus, *Haer.*, 1.7.5.

113. Origen comments (5.61) that Celsus means the Ebionites, though he may have reference to the Elkaisaites, another sect of Jewish Christians, mentioned by Eusebius, *Ecclesiastical History*, 6.38 (quoting from Origen's commentary on Ps. 82).

114. The Simonians flourished in Samaria and were probably a pre-Christian thaumaturgic sect. Whether they should be called "gnostic" is unclear; Irenaeus was the first to trace the gnostic heresy back to Simon the Magician (*Against Heresies* 1.23.1). In any case, they are remembered with an uncertain degree of accuracy in Acts 8.9–25 as representing a threat to the success of the gospel in Samaria.

115. The story is offered by Irenaeus (1.23.2), Tertullian (*De anima* 34), and Hippolytus (*Refut.* 6.19). Wilhelm Bousset analyzes the Helen tradition in *Die Hauptprobleme der Gnosis* (Goettingen, 1907), 78ff.

116. Both Irenaeus (*Against Heresies* 1.25.6) and Epiphanius (*Panarion* 27.6.1) mention Marcellina as being a follower of the Egyptian gnostic Carpocrates. She is thought to have come to Rome during the time of Anicetus' episcopate.

117. Salome figures in a number of gnostic works as being one of the Lord's apostles, notably in the *Gospel of Thomas* and the *Pistis Sophia*; Clement of Alexandria (*Miscellanies* 3.45.63, 66, 92) mentions her in connection with the *Gospel According to to the Egyptians*.

118. The Ophites honored Mariamne as being the apostle designated by James, the Lord's brother, to carry on his teaching (Hippolytus, *Refutation* 5.7.1; 10.9.3).

119. The extent of the hostility mentioned here by Celsus is also acknowledged by Christian writers such as Justin (1 *Apol.* 26).

120. Plato, *Epistles*, 7.341C.

121. Plato, *Epistles*, 7.341D. Celsus again calls the Christians to task for their lack of book-learning and their claim to have a superior wisdom. In the letter cited, Plato makes a distinction between the "true" and the "false" philosophical temperaments, the latter being "but a mere surface coloring of opinions penetrating, like sunburn, only skin deep" (7.340D). Celsus here pays tribute to the use of questions and answers as a means of arriving at the truth of a belief (cf. Plato, *Epistles*, 7.344B), and criticizes the Christians for their "immediate resort to faith" whenever challenged on some point of logic.

122. "For everything that exists there are three instruments by which the knowledge of it is necessarily imparted; fourth, there is the knowledge itself, and as fifth we must count the thing itself, which is known and truly exists" (Plato, *Ep.* 7.342A, B).

123. Origen (*Against Celsus* 6.11) replies that the Christian teachers "put the gospel before each man in a form suited to his character and condition. . . . There are indeed some to whom we preach only an exhortation to believe, since they are incapable of anything more; but with others, we do all that we can to approach them with rational arguments by questions and answers."

124. I Cor. 3.19.

125. Heracleitus, Frags. 78–79.

126. Plato, *Apology*, 20D. Celsus is here concerned with making a distinction between the self-professed *agnoia* of a philosopher in his search for wisdom and truth and the Christian idea that simplicity per se is virtuous.

127. Cf. *Against Celsus* 1.27 on the social structure of the Christian communities. See also A. J. Malherbe, *Social Aspects of Early Christianity* (Baton Rouge, La., 1977).

128. Plato, *Laws*, 715E. Celsus means to distinguish between reasonable humility and the self-abasement he thinks characterizes the Christian relationship between God and mankind as evidenced in the penitential system. Tertullian (*On Penitence* 9) describes practices similar to those known to Celsus. Theophrastus (*Char.* 16) and Plutarch (*Moralia* 166A) complain that *proskynesis* (prostration) is the mark of a superstitious mind.

129. Mark 6.2, and pars.

130. Plato, *Laws*, 743A. Celsus here reasserts what is by this point a familiar objection to Christianity, namely, that such "truth" as its doctrines may possess is unoriginal.

131. Plato, *Epistles*, 2.312E; and cf. Justin, 1 *Apology*, 1.60.7; Clement of Alexandria, *Strom.*, 5.103.1. The church fathers familiar with this

passage generally understood Plato to have adumbrated the Christian doctrine of the trinity.

132. Plato, *Phaedrus*, 247A.

133. See Franz Cumont, *Les Mysteres de Mithra* (Brussels, 1913), and Wilhelm Bousset, "Die Himmelreise der Seele," *Archiv für Religionswissenschaft*, 4 (1901) 136–69. Similarities between Mithraism and Christianity were observed by the church fathers from Justin onward; cf. I *Apol.* 66. Their reply to the familiar charge of "borrowing" from the mystery religions was that the devil, anticipating the foundation of the church, had caused the pagans to preempt Christian rites and doctrines.

134. The elaborate cosmology described here by Celsus is probably gnostic. The idea that this world is hemmed in by a great serpent, Leviathan (cf. Isa. 27.1; Job 3.8, etc.) was prevalent in gnostic Christian communities, as the evidence from the *Pistis Sophia* (126) and *Acts of Thomas* (32) makes clear.

135. See Matt. 5.22.

136. Of the possible parallels to this story cited by Chadwick (*Origen, Contra Celsum*, 6.27, note 2, p. 342), the closest appears to be a reference in the *Clementine Recognitions* (1.45) to the effect that the son of God is called "Christ" because "the Father anointed him with oil which was taken from the tree of life." It is unlikely that Origen is correct in saying that Celsus invented his information.

137. The division of angels mentioned by Celsus is known to Irenaeus as being a doctrine of the Gnostics (*Against Heresies* 1.30–2–3). Celsus shows himself to be particularly well versed in gnostic Christian doctrines, where the identification of the Old Testament God with an inferior angel is commonplace.

138. Gen. 3.14-15.

139. Cf. I Cor. 2.30.

140. Apparently Celsus has Marcionite polemic against the fickleness of the Old Testament God in mind (cf. Tertullian, *Against Marcion*, 1–3); but he confuses the position of Christians who opposed and would have eliminated the Old Testament books as being the revelation of an inferior god with that of Christians committed to an allegorical interpretation of the Hebrew scripture and who persevered in interpreting the "new" covenant as a further revelation of the God of Israel. Celsus offers the interesting observation that some Christians are simply hypocritical in their beliefs and accommodate their views to appease the Jews when expedient, and at other times, when called upon to defend the difference between Jewish law and Christian practice, argue that the God of the Jews and the Christian God are on-

tologically distinct beings. This is undoubtedly a simplification of the historical situation Celsus encountered; he is unable to make sense of the range of interpretations—some monotheistic, others not—in use in the various Christian communities known to him.

141. Tertullian, *Against Marcion*, 1.6.2. Tertullian suggests that Marcion has not postulated two supreme gods, but unequal gods: "the one a judge, fierce and warlike, the other mild and peaceable, solely kind and supremely good."

142. The gnostic system described is that of Valentinus; cf. Irenaeus, *Against Heresies*, 1.29.4; 30.3–9.

143. Herodotus 4.59.

144. Cf. Mark 16.9–20; Acts 3.6. Undoubtedly Paul is speaking of similar powers in I Cor. 2.4. The early Christians regarded such demonstrations as proof of doctrine; Celsus' description suggests that many Christian teachers of the second century attracted attention by means of conventional magic and sleight of hand, and Irenaeus knows of eucharistic celebrations of a specifically magical bent (cf. *Haer.* 1.12). Cf. also Smith, *Jesus the Magician* (New York, 1977).

145. The idea that magicians were morally depraved is widespread: see Plotinus, *Enneads*, 4.4.43–44; Porphyry, *Life of Plotinus*, 10.

146. Cf. II Thess. 2.3–5; Celsus shows some knowledge of Rev. 20.7: "When the thousand years are ended, Satan will be loosed from his prison and will come out to deceive the nations which are at the four corners of the earth."

147. Mark 13.5–6, pars.

148. Heracleitus, Frag. 80.

149. Pherecydes of Syros, Frag. 4.

150. Plutarch, *Moralia*, 371A, B.

151. *Iliad* 1.590f.

152. *Iliad* 15.18–24.

153. Pherecydes, Frag. 5. Celsus' argument centers on the right of a powerful god to punish arrogance by an outright demonstration of force; the Christians preach a god who made concessions to the devil, and so cannot be regarded as all-powerful.

154. Cf. Mark 8.34–35.

155. Celsus seems to have in mind the woes ascribed to Jesus in the Gospel of Matthew (24.13–36).

156. See Gen. 1–3. Origen's defense is that the writers of comedy wrote from a desire to make people laugh, whereas the purpose of Moses, in writing laws for the whole nation "was to encourage people to believe that they came from God." (*Cels. 6.49*).

157. Thus said the Marcionites (cf. Tertullian, *Against Marcion*, 1.22).

158. This line of argument is close to that offered by Irenaeus against Marcion: If the lot of mankind belongs to the Creator, then the supreme God becomes no more than a usurper of another's property (*Against Heresies* 4.33.2). See also Tertullian, *Against Marcion*, 3.4.4.

159. Gen. 6.6.

160. Gen. 4.23.

161. Celsus refers to the apparent contradiction between Gen. 1.3f. and 1.14–16.

162. Gen. 2.3.

163. Ps. 18.2; Isa. 4.20, etc. Origen argues that Christians are not anthropomorphic in their understanding of the Old Testament, but rather interpret such passages allegorically (*Cels.* 6.62).

164. John 1.1–18.

165. Plato argues (*Republic* 509B) that the Good exceeds essence. Celsus uses the Platonic doctrine to refute what he considers naive Jewish and Christian anthropomorphic ideas of the godhead.

166. *Republic* 518A: "Anyone who has common sense will remember that the bewilderments of the eyes are of two kinds and arise from two causes, either from coming out of the light or from going into the light, which is true of the mind's eye quite as much as of the bodily eye."

167. Cf. John 1.4–5.

168. Cf. Epictetus, *Discourses*, 1.14: "Are not our bodies so bound up and united with the whole, and are not our souls much more [bound up] and in contact with God as parts of him and portions of him, and does not God perceive every motion of these parts as being his own motion connate with himself?"

169. According to Tertullian, the divine afflatus was actually lodged in the virgin's womb by God's breathing into it (cf. *On the Flesh of Christ*).

170. Celsus refers to sects like the Marcionites, which denied the predictive character of Hebrew prophecy.

171. A literalist interpretation of Christian references to Isa. 52.14, "His face was so marred—more than any man's—and his form more than those of the sons of men," and Isa. 53.2–3: "He possessed no manner of beauty; when we look at him, we see nothing beautiful about him."

172. The prevalence of wandering prophets in Asia Minor is treated in a study by E. Fascher, *Prophetes* (Giessen, 1927), pp. 190ff.

173. Gen. 8.17.

174. Exod. 17.13–16; Num. 21.34–35, etc.

175. Deut. 1.26–45; 7.4.

176. Matt. 19.24; 20.25–27.

177. Matt. 6.26–29; 5.39.

178. *Odyssey* 4.563f.

179. *Phaedo*, 109A, B.

180. Celsus argues that the ongoing character of these revelations distinguishes them from the secret revelation of Jesus; he does not suggest that gods do not manifest themselves in human form.

181. Apparently a reference to the antidocetic passages in the gospels (e.g., John 20.27), or to Christian teachings based upon belief in the coequal humanity and divinity of Jesus.

182. Cf. Paul, II Cor. 5.16.

183. Celsus here alludes to the gnostic sect known as the Ophites: See Hippolytus, *Refutation*, 5; and Irenaeus, *Against Heresies*, 1.30.

184. Plato, *Timaeus*, 28C.

185. Cf. Plato, *Republic*, 508B.

186. Cicero, *Tuscan Orations*, 2.52.

187. Epictetus, *Discourses*, 1.8.14; 1.16.20.

188. Celsus obviously refers to Jesus' cry of despair from the cross; Mark 15.34. Here, as elsewhere, he challenges the divinity of Jesus on the grounds that he lacked the virtue of *apatheia* in the face of adversity.

189. Many Christian writers—Theophilus of Antioch, Clement of Alexandria, and Lactantius—quote freely from the Sybilline oracles, adapted, however, for Christian use.

190. Matt. 5.39.

191. Plato, *Crito*, 49B–E.

192. *Crito*, loc cit.

193. Most of what Celsus offers in this section is gleaned from reports in Herodotus 4.59, 188.

194. Heracleitus, Frag. 5.

195. Matt. 6.24.

196. This is the core of Celsus' attack on Christian iconoclasm and the inconsistency of the Christian position: If God is the creator of the world, then everything in the world belongs rightfully to him, and the worship of things in the world, including those gods that derive from him, must be accounted a good act. The Christians err, therefore, in denying honor to what belongs to God. Their error is compounded in their refusal to acknowledge custom: they are accused of cutting themselves off from the rest of mankind by their obstinance.

197. The withering charge here is that the Christians cannot be called monotheists, as they worship a man as a god. Such attacks as these stand behind later philosophical defenses of the unity of the godhead, and issue finally in the credal definitions of the fourth century.

198. Cf. Phil. 2.6–11.

199. Chadwick takes this mangled quotation, in part derived from Luke 22.38, as a gnosticized version of the story of the agony in Gethsemane.

200. Plato, *Phaedrus*, 247A; *Timaeus* 29E.

201. Paul anticipates Celsus' critique of Christian aversion to idol worship in I Corinthians 8.4–7. Celsus' point throughout this section, however, is that in perpetuating Jewish dietary observances and refraining from public festivals involving idol-worship, the Christians acknowledge the reality of other gods.

202. Cf. *Against Celsus* 3.41.

203. On magical effect of the name "Jesus" cf. Mark 16.17 and Phil. 2.10.

204. Celsus' example may not be mere hyperbole: cf. Minucius Felix, *Octavius*, 8.4, who comments that the pagan, Caecilius, was enraged at the sight of Christians spitting at the gods. Celsus argues that the Christians should be persuaded, if by nothing else, by the fact that they suffer for the profession of their faith, whereas those who worship the images scorned by the Christians enjoy peace and security.

205. Christian writers in the second century countered this criticism with "documentary" proof of various sorts, especially with the use of forged letters purported to have been written by those responsible for the execution of Jesus. Of these, the forged correspondence between Pilate and Tiberius is perhaps the most famous; see my *Jesus Outside the Gospels*, pp. 63–65.

206. Celsus' criticism is reflected in the apologetic section of the New Testament epistle known as II Peter: *"Pou estin hē epangelia tē parousias autou; aph' hēs gar hoi patres ekoimēthēsan panta houtos diamenei ap' archēs ktiseōs"* ["Where is the promise of his coming? For since the fathers died everything has continued in just the same way as it has been since the beginning."] The sentiment is assigned to the "scoffers" projected to appear in the last days.

207. Cf. II Peter 3.8–9.

208. Celsus derives this analysis of the origin of the soul from Plato, *Phaedo*, 114B, C; *Republic*, 517B.

209. Celsus' argument is that the Christian idea of martyrdom is really an absurd attempt to explain their humiliation: as they are under sentence of death for their behavior, they have made hatred of the body and of this world tenets of their religion. On the Christian perception of martyrdom, cf. Tertullian, *Apology*, 38.50.

210. Plato, *Theaetetus*, 176A.

211. On the Egyptian astrological divisions and their application, see W. Gundel, *Dekane und Dekansternbilder* (1936).

212. Phil. 2.11.
213. Cf. I Peter 2.13–14 (dating from the second century), and Titus 3.1.
214. The charge of atheism is a recurrent one; cf. Justin, 1 *Apology*, 6.
215. Homer, *Iliad*, 2.205.

BIBLIOGRAPHY

Andresen, Karl. *Logos und Nomos: Die Polemik des Kelsos wider das Christentum.* Berlin, 1955.

Bader, Robert. *Der Alēthēs Logos der Kelsos.* Stuttgart and Berlin, 1940.

Bail, P. *Die philosophische Fundamentierung von Celsus' Angriffes wider das Christentum.* Erlangen, 1921.

Bordes, Georg. "L'Apologétique d'Origène d'après le contre Celse." Diss., Univ. of Paris, 1900.

Borret, Marcel, ed. *Origenes, Contre Celse.* Introduction et texte critique. (Sources chrétiennes, nos. 132, 136, 147, 150.) Paris, 1967.

Bošnjak, Branko, *Grčka filozofska Biblije. Kelsos contra apologeticos.* Zagreb, 1971.

Chadwick, Henry. *Early Christian Thought and the Classical Tradition: Studies in Justin, Clement, and Origen.* New York, 1966.

_____, ed. and trans. *Origen, Contra Celsum.* Cambridge, Eng. 1953.

_____. "Origen, Celsus, and the Stoa," *Journal of Theological Studies,* 48 (1947), 34–49.

_____. "Origen, Celsus, and the Resurrection of the Body," *Harvard Theological Review,* 41 (1948), 83–102.

Crouzel, Henri. *Bibliographie critique d'Origène.* La Haye, 1971. (For secondary materials beyond 1971, the reader is referred to the *Bibliographia Patristica,* "Origenes," Berlin, 1971/1972 seq.)

_____. *Origène et la Philosophie.* Paris, 1962.

Denis, J. F. *Du discours de Celse contre les chrétiens intitulé "Le discours véritable."* N.d.; periodical extract in University of Michigan Library.

de Faye, Eugene. *Origen and His Work.* New York, 1929.

Geffcken, J. *Der Ausgang des griechisch-römischen Heidentums.* Heidelberg, 1920–29.

Glöckner, Otto. *Celsi Alēthēs Logos, excussit et restituere conatus est.* Bonn, 1924.

Hanson, R. P. C. *Allegory and Event: A Study of the Sources and Significance of Origen's Interpretation of Scripture.* London, 1959.

Harris, J. Rendel. *Celsus and Aristides.* Manchester, 1922. Rpt. from the *Bulletin of the John Rylands Library,* 6 (1922), 163–75.

Heine, Otto. "Ueber Celsus' 'Alēthēs Logos,'" in *Philologische Abhandlungen Martin Hertz dargebracht,* 1888, pp. 197–214.

Koch, Hal. *Pronoia und Paideusis, Studien über Origenes und sein Verhältnis zum Platonismus.* Leipzig, 1932.

Koetschau, Paul. *Die Textüberlieferung der Bücher des Origenes gegen Celsus in der handschriften dieses Werkes und der Philokalia.* Leipzig, 1889.

de Lange, N. R. M. *Origen and the Jews: Studies in Jewish-Christian Relations in Third-Century Palestine.* Cambridge, Eng., 1976.

Lods, M. "Étude sur les sources juives de la polémique de Celse contre les chrétiens," *Revue d'histoire et de philosophie religieuses,* 21 (1941), 1–31.

Miura-Stange, A. *Celsus und Origenes.* Giessen, 1929.

Muth, J. F. S. *Der Kampf des heidenischen Philosophen Celsus gegen das Christentum.* Mainz, 1899.

Nautin, Pierre. *Origène, sa vie et son ouvre.* Paris, 1977.

Patrick, John. *The Apology of Origen in Reply to Celsus: A Chapter in the History of Apologetics.* Edinburgh, 1892.

Robinson, J. Armitage. *The Philocalia of Origen.* Cambridge, Eng., 1893.

Rougier, L. A. P. *Celse ou le conflit de la civilisation antique et du christianisme primitif.* Paris, 1926.

Pelagaud, Elysée. *Un conservateur au second siècle: étude sur Celse et la première escarmouche entre la philosophie antique et le christianisme naissant.* Lyon, 1878.

Turner, W. "Celsus: The Voltaire of the Second Century," *Irish Theological Quarterly,* 3 (1908), 137–50.

Weber, Karl Otto. *Origenes de Neuplatoniker: Versuch einer Interpretation.* Munich, 1962.

800019

800